Epicurus: Life Reflections
Letter to Menoeceus
&
Principle Doctrines

Diogenes Laërtius
Life of Epicurus

Edited and with an Introduction by
Babette Babich
Translation by R.D. Hicks

First published 2018 by

NNS Press
113 West 60th Street, 925H
NY, NY 10023

Babette Babich has asserted her right under the Copyright, Designs and Patent Act, 1988 to be identified as the author of this work.

Introduction and photographs.

All rights reserved.

Library of Congress cataloguing of the print edition in progress.

Babich, Babette, 1956–

Epicurus: Life Reflections. Letter to Menoeceus and Principle Doctrines.
Diogenes Laërtius: Life of Epicurus

NNS Press
New York City, NY

ISBN-13: 978-1-949766-01-1

Table of Contents

Introduction i

Epicurus, *Letter to Menoecus* 1

Epicurus, *Principle Doctrines* 9

Diogenes Laërtius, *Epicurus* 17

Introduction

Introduction

Life Reflections: From Epicurus to Nietzsche

Epicurus was born on the isle of Samos in 341 BCE, the son of Neocles, a native Athenian. Epicurus travelled to Athens in 323 BCE to register as a citizen and to complete those military responsibilities exigent upon Athenian youth at the (classical) age of 18. He left Athens after a year in order to join his father in Colophon subsequent to the expulsion of the colonists from Samos. A contemporary of Zeno, Epicurus claimed to have been self-taught.[1] He began to teach philosophy in Mytilene in 310 BCE which led to tensions compelling his departure, whereupon he established a school in Lampsacus, ultimately returning to Athens in 306 BCE. A sickly man, Epicurus was never robust and suffered from digestive and other internal troubles. He died in Athens, in 270 BCE.

We know a great deal of what we know about Epicurus given Diogenes Laërtius, *Lives of Eminent Philosophers* (see the third chapter below), and here, I am indebted to both Friedrich Nietzsche's and R. D. Hicks' account of Epicurus. Hicks himself depends on Hermann Usener's

---

[1] This is in clear contradiction to Epicurus' dependence on forebears such as Anaxagoras in addition to Xenophanes and, above all, the atomist philosophy of Democritus. See for a discussion of the last, Pamela M. Huby, "Epicurus' Attitude to Democritus," *Phronesis*, Vol. 23, No. 1 (1978): 80-86.

Epicurea.² Epicurus was also important for Dante and in antiquity, albeit more critically, for Cicero along with Seneca, and Lucretius celebrated Epicurus in his *De rerum Natura*. Epicurus is thus a fairly Roman Greek.³

The texts from Epicurus to follow, all in the public domain, were translated by the blind Cambridge classicist, Robert Drew Hicks (1850–1929), who also translated, with the assistance of Sir Thomas Heath, the Loeb edition of Diogenes Laërtius' *Lives*.

Epicurus was a popular teacher, given to mocking his competitors, not at all surprising given the temper of the times, the New Comedy, but also given the substance of his teaching. Epicurus' cosmology, indebted as noted above to Democritus, and which, going forward we also encounter in Lucretius, was of a piece with his moral philosophy, a neatly coordinate unity that appealed to many followers.⁴

Epicurus appeal continues with his straightforward focus on sense observation, avoidance of myth, and simple reasoning, in addition to a flexible notion of the

---

² Hermann Usener, *Epicurea* (Leipzig: Teubner, 1887). Cf. Cyril B. Bailey, *Epicurus: The Extant Remains* (Oxford: Clarendon Press, 1926).
³ See Michael Erler, "Epicureanism in the Roman Empire" in James Warren, ed, *The Cambridge Companion to Epicureanism* (Cambridge: Cambridge University Press, 2009), pp. 46-64 and see, too, Malcolm Schofield's review: "Epicureanism and Politics," *The Classical Review New Series*, Vol. 57, No. 1 (2007): 179-181. And, despite general scholastic condemnations, this can even be extended to the Church. Seem Richard P. Jungkuntz, "Christian Approval of Epicureanism," *Church History*, Vol. 31, No. 3 (Sep., 1962), pp. 279-293.
⁴ See for an overall summary account, Diskin Clay, *Paradosis & Survival* (Ann Arbor: University of Michigan Press, 1998). And more recently, Attila Németh's *Epicurus on the Self* (New York: Routledge, 2017).

παρέγκλισις [Lucretius: *clinamen*], or swerve. In France, Epicurus' cosmological thought influenced the thought of Henri Bergson, Gilles Deleuze, Michel Serres, and Michel Onfray along with contemporary Anglophone philosophers interested in what today's analytic philosophy names 'naturalism.' In moral philosophy, Epicurus inspired Mill and Bentham.[5] And, in political philosophy, Karl Marx wrote his doctoral dissertation on Epicurus and Democritus.[6]

Epicurus was the author of some 300 written works, and Diogenes Laërtius lists thirty-seven books, numbers which ought to inspire caution in offering summary accounts concerning the range of his teachings. At the same time, his school inspired an virtual industry of commentary and summary, especially given extensive citation in Diogenes Laërtius as seen below. To this extent, we may be inspired by his thought on nature in addition to his epistolary, and thus effectively personal reflections on life and death, life conduct in general or ethics as well as his apothegmatic 'principle doctrines.' It is routinely noted that Epicurus as leader or hero of his school, instituted a customary feast on his birthday, that is, the 10th of Gamelion month (approximately our

---

[5] See, for discussion, Julia Annas, "Epicurus on Pleasure and Happiness." *Philosophical Topics. Ancient Greek Philosophy*, Vol. 15, No. 2 (Fall 1987): 5-21 and Geoffrey Scarre, "Epicurus as a Forerunner of Utilitarianism," *Utilitas*, Vol. 6, Iss. 2 (November 1994): 219-231.

[6] See for an English translation, Karl Marx, *The Difference Between the Democritean and Epicurean Philosophy of Nature* (Moscow: Progress Publishers, 1902 [1841]). See for a recent analysis, James Warren's *Epicurus and Democritean Ethics: An Archaeology of Ataraxia* (Cambridge: Cambridge University Press, 2002).

January), although Hicks reminds us that his actual birthday was likely to have been a few days earlier.

Hicks summarily cites Usener, *Epicurea*: "Epicurus defined philosophy 'as a daily business of speech and thought to secure a happy life.'"⁷

Happiness — this becomes the foundation of *Utilitarianism* — is defined negatively and therefore precisely as freedom from pain. The goal of philosophy is happiness; happiness is the absence of suffering. The appeal of this definition is immediately compounded by the complexity of the teaching itself as this involves not only a number of reflexive arguments but traditionally epitomized in brief summaries, including, most concisely, the famous *Tetrapharmakos* summarized in Philodemus, *To the Friends of the School* —

1. Don't fear the gods
2. Don't worry about death
3. What is good is easy to get
4. What is terrible is easy to endure⁸

The brevity of these counsels secures their appeal.

And Friedrich Nietzsche in the 1879 text, *The Wanderer and His Shadow*, published as the second part of the second volume of *Human, All too Human* in 1886, offers his own summary of Epicurus' teachings in a word fresco — one is not surprised to learn that Epicurus' sayings were carved on the walls, so that his teachings

---

⁷ Usener, *Epicurea*, Fr. 219, p. 169.
⁸ See Philodemus, *To the Friends of the School* [*Pros tous hetairous*] in: A.A. Long and David Sedley, *The Hellenistic Philosophers* (Cambridge: Cambridge University Press, 1987), p. 25.

might be recovered in this way.⁹ Like Epicurus' own doctrine, Nietzsche's aphorism is concise, perfect in its imagery: "— A garden, figs, little cheeses, and to that three or four good friends — that was the opulence of Epicurus." (WS §193)

Stylistically, Nietzsche's aphorism offers us a brief commentary on the nature of luxury. Is that all it takes? Just a little garden? Some figs, small cheese a few friends? Such a little list invites one to imagine that opulence so defined, this very idea of sufficiency, what is enough and what might count as such, when you think about it, would be available to almost everyone — one is reminded that in addition to women, slaves too were also to be counted in Epicurus's school. And if available to almost everyone, also possible, at any time. Reflection on this small list of requisites invites us to see their ultimate value. For just how is one to live such that one comes by a garden? This would have been a special achievement in a city, for Epicurus, Athens. For us today that might be Paris or London or New York. Figs, to be sure, remind us of the seasons and the relevance of the ripeness of time (for Nietzsche was also fond of commenting on the significance of figs, a metaphor for fulfilled and passing time, and that also entails foresight, preservation, as the figs can be fresh, just to go with the cheese, or dried figs, as these might better suit the specified *little cheeses*, not any cheese then, a Marcellin, an *époisse* maybe, a little *crottin* wrapped in a certain leaf (of asphodel no less — corresponding to the same

---

⁹ See R. D. Hicks, "Epicurus and Hedonism" in: *Stoic and Epicurean* (New York: C. Scribner's Sons, 1910), here p. 104.

powdered root mentioned by Professor Severus Snape in J.K. Rowling's *Harry Potter and the Philosopher's Stone* which happens to include an allusion to Homer and the fields of the dead in Elysium),[10] which leaf, in the case of little wrapped cheeses, dries out just at the moment when the cheese has passed its prime (which again underscores the value of the very little, in terms of time of the cheese itself, all of which thus can underscore the brevity of, that is also the luxury of life). All of this comes under *meteorology*, as Howard Caygill tells us, and as is plain today: presupposing good weather.[11]

In addition, there are the friends. This requirement was an elusive one, as Nietzsche reflected constantly, borrowing Montaigne's reflections on the nature of the friend.[12] And reflection on Epicurus' list tells us to keep the count sparing: three or four, not more. The emphasis is minimalism.

No item in Epicurus' listing turns out to be dispensable — the little bit in question is of the essence and the achievement of taking all these together, the essence of opulence. This is luxury. One wants to add, *true luxury* just to the extent that so much of what we ordinarily take to be luxury is excess: superfluous, too much.

---

[10] See for references, Babette Babich, "Spirit and Grace, Letters and Voice," *Journal of the Philosophy of Education*, III (2018): 1-27, here pp. 8 and 18.
[11] Howard Caygill, "Under Epicurean Skies," *Angelaki, Journal of the Theoretical Humanities*, Vol. 11, no. 3 (December 2006): 107-115.
[12] See here Suzanne Stern-Gillet, "Epicurus and Friendship," *Dialogue*, Vol. 28, Issue 2 (1989): 275-288 and J. M. Rist, "The Problem of Friendship" in *Epicurus: An Introduction* (Cambridge: Cambridge University Press, 1972), pp. 127-140 as well as Babich, "Nietzsche's Imperative as a Friend's Encomium: On Becoming the One You Are, Ethics, and Blessing," *Nietzsche-Studien*, 33 (2003): 29-58. On Montaigne, himself influenced by Epicurus, see Alexander Nehamas, *On Friendship* (New York: Basic Books, 2016).

Thus Nietzsche's formula, again, slicing between the typographic dashes the Germans call thoughtslashes, *Gedankenstriche*: "— A garden, figs, little cheeses, and to that three or four good friends —" (WS §193), tells us that this is all one needs, indeed, if it can be attained. We can go on to read Nietzsche's 19th century reflections *"The simple life,"* and in our 21st century this would be even truer:

> Nowadays a simple mode of life is difficult: it requires much more reflection and inventive talent than is possessed by very clever people. (WS §196)

Nietzsche's aphorism to follow comments further on Epicurus in *"The Epochs of Life,"* highlighting, and now we can see the relevance of Epicurus' cosmological theory for his life principles, the very cyclical return of satisfaction and desire, highlighting consummation or fulfilment, which one may read as a reflexive test of the former aphorism. As Nietzsche epitomizes perfection: "Here one has attained a state of satisfaction. All else is hunger and thirst — or satiety." (WS §193)

All we need is the still point of simplicity but — like the small garden, like the figs and little cheeses, with a few friends — acquiring the small, the little, the few, is no easy thing. For that we need, and have, philosophy.

— Babette Babich
Winchester, England
18 August 2018

Epicurus

Letter to Menoeceus

&

Principle Doctrines

Epicurus

Letter to Menoeceus

Greetings!

Let no one be slow to seek wisdom when he is young nor weary in the search thereof when he is grown old. For no age is too early or too late for the health of the soul. And to say that the season for studying philosophy has not yet come, or that it is past and gone, is like saying that the season for happiness is not yet or that it is now no more. Therefore, both old and young ought to seek wisdom, the former in order that, as age comes over him, he may be young in good things because of the grace of what has been, and the latter in order that, while he is young, he may at the same time be old, because he has no fear of the things which are to come. So we must exercise ourselves in the things which bring happiness, since, if that be present, we have everything, and, if that be absent, all our actions are directed toward attaining it.

Those things which without ceasing I have declared to you, those do, and exercise yourself in those, holding them to be the elements of right life. First believe that God is a living being immortal and happy, according to the notion of a god indicated by the common sense of humankind; and so of him anything that is at agrees not with about him whatever may uphold both his happiness and his immortality. For truly there are gods, and knowledge of them is evident; but they are not such as the multitude believe, seeing that people do not steadfastly maintain the notions they form respecting them. Not the person who denies the gods worshipped by the multitude, but he who affirms of the gods what the multitude believes about them is truly impious. For the utterances of the multitude about the gods are not true preconceptions but false assumptions; hence it is that the greatest evils happen to the wicked and the greatest blessings happen to the good from the hand of the gods, seeing that they are always favorable to their own good qualities and take pleasure in people like to themselves, but reject as alien whatever is not of their kind.

Accustom yourself to believe that death is nothing to us, for good and evil imply awareness, and death is the privation of all awareness; therefore a right understanding that death is nothing to us makes the mortality of life enjoyable, not by adding to life an unlimited time, but by taking away the yearning after immortality. For life has no terror; for those who thoroughly apprehend that there are no terrors for them in ceasing to live. Foolish, therefore, is the person who says that he fears death, not because it will pain when it comes, but because it pains in the prospect. Whatever causes no annoyance when it is present, causes only a groundless pain in the expectation. Death, therefore, the most awful of evils, is nothing to us, seeing that, when we are, death is not come, and, when death is come, we are not. It is nothing, then, either to the living or to the dead, for with the living it is not and the dead exist no longer. But in the world, at one time people shun death as the greatest of all evils, and at another time choose it as a respite from the evils in life. The wise person does not deprecate life nor does he fear the cessation of life. The thought of life is no offense to him, nor is the cessation of life regarded as an evil. And even as people choose of food not merely and simply the larger portion, but the more pleasant, so the wise seek to enjoy the time which is most pleasant and not merely that which is longest. And he who admonishes the young to live well and the old to make a good end speaks foolishly, not merely because of the desirability of life, but because the same exercise at once teaches to live well and to die well. Much worse is he who says that it were good not to be born, but when once one is born to pass with all speed through the gates of Hades. For if he truly believes this, why does he not depart from life? It were easy for him to do so, if once he were firmly convinced. If he speaks only in mockery, his words are foolishness, for those who hear believe him not.

We must remember that the future is neither wholly ours nor wholly not ours, so that neither must we count upon it as quite certain to come nor despair of it as quite certain not to come.

We must also reflect that of desires some are natural, others are groundless; and that of the natural some are necessary as well as natural, and some natural only. And of the necessary desires some are necessary if we are to be happy, some if the body is to be rid of uneasiness, some if we are even to live. He who has a clear and certain understanding of these things will direct every preference and aversion toward securing health of body and tranquillity of mind, seeing that this is the sum and end of a happy life. For the end of all our actions is to be free from pain and fear, and, when once we have attained all this, the tempest of the soul is laid; seeing that the living creature has no need to go in search of something that is lacking, nor to look anything else by which the good of the soul and of the body will be fulfilled. When we are pained pleasure, then, and then only, do we feel the need of pleasure. For this reason we call pleasure the alpha and omega of a happy life. Pleasure is our first and kindred good. It is the starting-point of every choice and of every aversion, and to it we come back, inasmuch as we make feeling the rule by which to judge of every good thing. And since pleasure is our first and native good, for that reason we do not choose every pleasure whatever, but often pass over many pleasures when a greater annoyance ensues from them. And often we consider pains superior to pleasures when submission to the pains for a long time brings us as a consequence a greater pleasure. While therefore all pleasure because it is naturally akin to us is good, not all pleasure is worthy of choice, just as all pain is an evil and yet not all pain is to be shunned. It is, however, by measuring one against another, and by looking at the conveniences and inconveniences, teat all these matters must be judged. Sometimes we treat the good as an evil, and the evil, on the contrary, as a good. Again, we regard independence of outward things as a great good, not so as in all cases to use little, but so as to be contented with little if we have not much, being honestly persuaded that they have the sweetest enjoyment of luxury who stand least in need of it, and that whatever is natural is easily procured and only the vain and worthless hard to win. Plain fare gives as much pleasure as a costly diet, when one the pain of want has been removed, while bread an water confer the highest possible pleasure when they are brought to hungry lips. To habituate one's se therefore, to simple and inexpensive diet supplies al that is needful for health, and enables a person to meet the necessary requirements of life without shrinking and it places us in a better condition when we approach at intervals a costly fare and renders us fearless of fortune.

When we say, then, that pleasure is the end and aim, we do not mean the pleasures of the prodigal or the pleasures of sensuality, as we are understood to do by some through ignorance, prejudice, or willful misrepresentation. By pleasure we mean the absence of pain in the body and of trouble in the soul. It is not an unbroken succession of drinking-bouts and of merrymaking, not sexual love, not the enjoyment of the fish and other delicacies of a luxurious table, which produce a pleasant life; it is sober reasoning, searching out the grounds of every choice and avoidance, and banishing those beliefs through which the greatest disturbances take possession of the soul. Of all this the end is prudence. For this reason prudence is a more precious thing even than the other virtues, for a life of pleasure which is not also a life of prudence, honor, and justice; nor lead a life of prudence, honor, and justice, which is not also a life of pleasure. For the virtues have grown into one with a pleasant life, and a pleasant life is inseparable from them.

Who, then, is superior in your judgment to such a person? He holds a holy belief concerning the gods, and is altogether free from the fear of death. He has diligently considered the end fixed by nature, and understands how easily the limit of good things can be reached and attained, and how either the duration or the intensity of evils is but slight. Destiny which some introduce as sovereign over all things, he laughs to scorn, affirming rather that some things happen of necessity, others by chance, others through our own agency. For he sees that necessity destroys responsibility and that chance or fortune is inconstant; whereas our own actions are free, and it is to them that praise and blame naturally attach. It were better, indeed, to accept the legends of the gods than to bow beneath destiny which the natural philosophers have imposed. The one holds out some faint hope that we may escape if we honor the gods, while the necessity of the naturalists is deaf to all entreaties. Nor does he hold chance to be a god, as the world in general does, for in the acts of a god there is no disorder; nor to be a cause, though an uncertain one, for he believes that no good or evil is dispensed by chance to people so as to make life happy, though it supplies the starting-point of great good and great evil. He believes that the misfortune of the wise is better than the prosperity of the fool. It is better, in short, that what is well judged in action should not owe its successful issue to the aid of chance.

Exercise yourself in these and kindred precepts day and night, both by yourself and with him who is like to you; then never, either in waking or in dream, will you be disturbed, but will live as a god among people. For people lose all appearance of mortality by living in the midst of immortal blessings.

Epicurus

Principal Doctrines

1. A happy and eternal being has no trouble himself and brings no trouble upon any other being; hence he is exempt from movements of anger and partiality, for every such movement implies weakness

2. Death is nothing to us; for the body, when it has been resolved into its elements, has no feeling, and that which has no feeling is nothing to us.

3. The magnitude of pleasure reaches its limit in the removal of all pain. When pleasure is present, so long as it is uninterrupted, there is no pain either of body or of mind or of both together.

4. Continuous pain does not last long in the body; on the contrary, pain, if extreme, is present a short time, and even that degree of pain which barely outweighs pleasure in the body does not last for many days together. Illnesses of long duration even permit of an excess of pleasure over pain in the body.

5. It is impossible to live a pleasant life without living wisely and well and justly, and it is impossible to live wisely and well and justly without living pleasantly. Whenever any one of these is lacking, when, for instance, the person is not able to live wisely, though he lives well and justly, it is impossible for him to live a pleasant life.

6. In order to obtain security from other people any means whatever of procuring this was a natural good.

7. Some people have sought to become famous and renowned, thinking that thus they would make themselves secure against their fellow-humans. If, then, the life of such persons really was secure, they attained natural good; if, however, it was insecure, they have not attained the end which by nature's own prompting they originally sought.

8. No pleasure is in itself evil, but the things which produce certain pleasures entail annoyances many times greater than the pleasures themselves.

9. If all pleasure had been capable of accumulation, — if this had gone on not only be recurrences in time, but all over the frame or, at any rate, over the principal parts of human nature, there would never have been any difference between one pleasure and another, as in fact there is.

10. If the objects which are productive of pleasures to profligate persons really freed them from fears of the mind, — the fears, I mean, inspired by celestial and atmospheric phenomena, the fear of death, the fear of pain; if, further, they taught them to limit their desires, we should never have any fault to find with such persons, for they would then be filled with pleasures to overflowing on all sides and would be exempt from all pain, whether of body or mind, that is, from all evil.

11. If we had never been molested by alarms at celestial and atmospheric phenomena, nor by the misgiving that death somehow affects us, nor by neglect of the proper limits of pains and desires, we should have had no need to study natural science.

12. It would be impossible to banish fear on matters of the highest importance, if a person did not know the nature of the whole universe, but lived in dread of what the legends tell us. Hence without the study of nature there was no enjoyment of unmixed pleasures.

13. There would be no advantage in providing security against our fellow humans, so long as we were alarmed by occurrences over our heads or beneath the earth or in general by whatever happens in the boundless universe.

14. When tolerable security against our fellow humans is attained, then on a basis of power sufficient to afford supports and of material prosperity arises in most genuine form the security of a quiet private life withdrawn from the multitude.

15. Nature's wealth at once has its bounds and is easy to procure; but the wealth of vain fancies recedes to an infinite distance.

16. Fortune but seldom interferes with the wise person; his greatest and highest interests have been, are, and will be, directed by reason throughout the course of his life.

17. The just person enjoys. the greatest peace of mind, while the unjust is full of the utmost disquietude.

18. Pleasure in the body admits no increase when once the pain of want has been removed; after that it only admits of variation. The limit of pleasure in the mind, however, is reached when we reflect on the things themselves and their congeners which cause the mind the greatest alarms.

19. Unlimited time and limited time afford an equal amount of pleasure, if we measure the limits of that pleasure by reason.

20. The body receives as unlimited the limits of pleasure; and to provide it requires unlimited time. But the mind, grasping in thought what the end and limit of the body is, and banishing the terrors of futurity, procures a complete and perfect life, and has no longer any need of unlimited time. Nevertheless it does not shun pleasure, and even in the hour of death, when ushered out of existence by circumstances, the mind does not lack enjoyment of the best life.

21. He who understands the limits of life knows how easy it is to procure enough to remove the pain of want and make the whole of life complete and perfect. Hence he has no longer any need of things which are not to be won save by labor and conflict.

22. We must take into account as the end all that really exists and all clear evidence of sense to which we refer our opinions; for otherwise everything will be full of uncertainty and confusion.

23. If you fight against all your sensations, you will have no standard to which to refer, and thus no means of judging even those judgments which you pronounce false.

24. If you reject absolutely any single sensation without stopping to discriminate with respect to that which awaits confirmation between matter of opinion and that which is already present, whether in sensation or in feelings or in any immediate perception of the mind, you will throw into confusion even the rest of your sensations by your groundless belief and so you will be rejecting the standard of truth altogether. If in your ideas based upon opinion you hastily affirm as true all that awaits confirmation as well as that which does not, you will not escape error, as you will be maintaining complete ambiguity whenever it is a case of judging between right and wrong opinion.

25. If you do not on every separate occasion refer each of your actions to the end prescribed by nature, but instead of this in the act of choice or avoidance swerve aside to some other end, your acts will not be consistent with your theories.

26. All such desires as lead to no pain when they remain ungratified are unnecessary, and the longing is easily got rid of, when the thing desired is difficult to procure or when the desires seem likely to produce harm.

27. Of all the means which are procured by wisdom to ensure happiness throughout the whole of life, by far the most important is the acquisition of friends.

28. The same conviction which inspires confidence that nothing we have to fear is eternal or even of long duration, also enables us to see that even in our limited conditions of life nothing enhances our security so much as friendship.

29. Of our desires some are natural and necessary others are natural, but not necessary; others, again, are neither natural nor necessary, but are due to illusory opinion.

30. Those natural desires which entail no pain when not gratified, though their objects are vehemently pursued, are also due to illusory opinion; and when they are not got rid of, it is not because of their own nature, but because of the person's illusory opinion.

31. Natural justice is a symbol or expression of usefullness, to prevent one person from harming or being harmed by another.

32. Those animals which are incapable of making covenants with one another, to the end that they may neither inflict nor suffer harm, are without either justice or injustice. And those tribes which either could not or would not form mutual covenants to the same end are in like case.

33. There never was an absolute justice, but only an agreement made in reciprocal association in whatever localities now and again from time to time, providing against the infliction or suffering of harm.

34. Injustice is not in itself an evil, but only in its consequence, viz. the terror which is excited by

apprehension that those appointed to punish such offenses will discover the injustice.

35. It is impossible for the person who secretly violates any article of the social compact to feel confident that he will remain undiscovered, even if he has already escaped ten thousand times; for right on to the end of his life he is never sure he will not be detected.

36. Taken generally, justice is the same for all, to wit, something found useful in mutual association; but in its application to particular cases of locality or conditions of whatever kind, it varies under different circumstances.

37. Among the things accounted just by conventional law, whatever in the needs of mutual association is attested to be useful, is thereby stamped as just, whether or not it be the same for all; and in case any law is made and does not prove suitable to the usefulness of mutual association, then this is no longer just. And should the usefulness which is expressed by the law vary and only for a time correspond with the prior conception, nevertheless for the time being it was just, so long as we do not trouble ourselves about empty words, but look simply at the facts.

38. Where without any change in circumstances the conventional laws, when judged by their consequences, were seen not to correspond with the notion of justice, such laws were not really just; but wherever the laws have ceased to be useful in consequence of a change in circumstances, in that case the laws were for the time

being just when they were useful for the mutual association of the citizens, and subsequently ceased to be just when they ceased to be useful.

39. He who best knew how to meet fear of external foes made into one family all the creatures he could; and those he could not, he at any rate did not treat as aliens; and where he found even this impossible, he avoided all association, and, so far as was useful, kept them at a distance.

40. Those who were best able to provide themselves with the means of security against their neighbors, being thus in possession of the surest guarantee, passed the most agreeable life in each other's society; and their enjoyment of the fullest intimacy was such that, if one of them died before his time, the survivors did not mourn his death as if it called for sympathy.

Diogenes Laërtius

Life of Epicurus

Life of Epicurus
From: Diogenes Laërtius
Lives of the Eminent Philosophers, Book X

1. Epicurus, son of Neocles and Chaerestrate, was a citizen of Athens of the deme Gargettus, and, as Metrodorus says in his book *On Noble Birth*, of the family of the Philaidae. He is said by Heraclides[13] in his *Epitome* of Sotion, as well as by other authorities, to have been brought up at Samos after the Athenians had sent settlers there and to have come to Athens at the age of eighteen, at the time when Xenocrates was lecturing at the Academy and Aristotle in Chalcis. Upon the death of Alexander of Macedon and the expulsion of the Athenian settlers from Samos by Perdiccas,[14] Epicurus left Athens to join his father in Colophon.

2. For some time he stayed there and gathered disciples, but returned to Athens in the archonship of Anaxicrates. [307-306 B.C.] And for a while, it is said, he prosecuted his studies in common with the other philosophers, but afterwards put forward independent views by the foundation of the school called after him. He says himself that he first came into contact with philosophy at the age of fourteen. Apollodorus the Epicurean, in the first book of his *Life of Epicurus*, says that he turned to philosophy in disgust at the schoolmasters who could not tell him the meaning of "chaos" in Hesiod.[15]

---
[13] i.e. Heraclides Lembos (F.H.G. iii. p. 70).
[14] Diod. Sic. xviii. 18. 9.
[15] Cf. Sext. Emp. *Adv. math.* x. 18, where the story is well told.

According to Hermippus, however, he started as a schoolmaster, but on coming across the works of Democritus turned eagerly to philosophy.

3. Hence the point of Timon's allusion [Fr. 51D] in the lines:

> Again there is the latest and most shameless of the physicists, the schoolmaster's son[16] from Samos, himself the most uneducated of mortals.

At his instigation his three brothers, Neocles, Chaeredemus, and Aristobulus, joined in his studies, according to Philodemus the Epicurean in the tenth book of his comprehensive work *On Philosophers*; furthermore his slave named Mys, as stated by Myronianus in his *Historical Parallels*. Diotimus[17] the Stoic, who is hostile to him, has assailed him with bitter slanders, adducing fifty scandalous letters as written by Epicurus; and so too did the author who ascribed to Epicurus the epistles commonly attributed to Chrysippus.

4. They are followed by Posidonius the Stoic and his school, and Nicolaus and Sotion in the twelfth book of his work entitled *Dioclean Refutations*, consisting of twenty-four books; also by Dionysius of Halicarnassus. They allege that he used to go round with his mother to

---

[16] The meaning is: "a schoolmaster like his father before him." Cf. Dem. De cor. 258 ἅματῷ πατρὶ πρὸς τῷ διδασκαλείῳ προσεδρεύων. From Aristophanes, *Acharn*. 595-7, it seems that patronymics were used of persons engaged in hereditary occupations.

[17] One Diotimus who calumniated Epicurus and was answered by the Epicurean Zeno is mentioned by Athenaeus, xiii. 611 B, as having been put to death.

cottages and read charms, and assist his father in his school for a pitiful fee;[18] further, that one of his brothers was a pander and lived with Leontion the courtesan; that he put forward as his own the doctrines of Democritus about atoms and of Aristippus about pleasure; that he was not a genuine Athenian citizen, a charge brought by Timocrates and by Herodotus in a book *On the Training of Epicurus as a Cadet*; that he basely flattered Mithras,[19] the minister of Lysimachus, bestowing on him in his letters Apollo's titles of Healer and Lord.

5. Furthermore that he extolled Idomeneus, Herodotus, and Timocrates, who had published his esoteric doctrines, and flattered them for that very reason. Also that in his letters he wrote to Leontion, "O Lord Apollo, my dear little Leontion, with what tumultuous applause we were inspired as we read your letter." Then again to Themista, the wife of Leonteus: "I am quite ready, if you do not come to see me, to spin thrice on my own axis and be propelled to any place that you, including Themista, agree upon"; and to the beautiful Pythocles he writes: "I will sit down and await thy divine advent, my heart's desire." And, as Theodorus says in the fourth book of his work, *Against Epicurus*, in another letter to Themista he thinks he preaches to her.[20]

---

[18] Compare again Dem. De cor. 258.
[19] Mithras was a Syrian. Cf. Plut. *Contra Epic.* 1097 b; *Adv. Col.* 1126 e.
[20] A perplexing passage. (1) As παραινετική is for the Stoics that branch of ethics which makes personal application of moral principles, the mss. may be right. (2) By changing αὐτῇ to αὐτήν, a little more sting is given to this tame remark: "he thinks that she preaches." (3) If this is one of the fifty

6. It is added that he corresponded with many courtesans, and especially with Leontion, of whom Metrodorus also was enamoured. It is observed too that in his treatise *On the Ethical End* he writes in these terms:[21] "I know not how to conceive the good, apart from the pleasures of taste, sexual pleasures, the pleasures of sound and the pleasures of beautiful form." And in his letter to Pythocles: "Hoist all sail, my dear boy, and steer clear of all culture." Epictetus calls him preacher of effeminacy and showers abuse on him.

Again there was Timocrates, the brother of Metrodorus, who was his disciple and then left the school. He in the book entitled Merriment asserts that Epicurus vomited twice a day from over-indulgence, and goes on to say that he himself had much ado to escape from those notorious midnight philosophizings and the confraternity with all its secrets;

7. further, that Epicurus's acquaintance with philosophy was small and his acquaintance with life even smaller;

---

scandalous letters alluded to in 3, Froben's αὐτὴν περαίνειν, which Bignone and Apelt adopt, may be right. (4) If emend we must, a rude remark is quite as probable as a compliment, cf. 8. Hence νομίζει αὐτὴν παρακινεῖν, "he deems her mad," if she says or thinks so-and-so, would be in the master's blunt manner, and Themista (to use the language of Phaedrus, 249 d) νουθετεῖται ὡς παρακινοῦσα.

[21] Cf. Athen. xii. 546 e, who cites the concluding words more fully thus: καὶτὰς διὰ μορφῆς κατ' ὄψιν ἡδείας κινήσεις· also vii. 280 a and, for a shorter version than that of D. L., vii. 278 f. Cf. also Cic. *Tusc. Disp.* iii. 41. The last words have been taken to refer especially to the pleasures afforded by music and again by painting and the plastic arts. But perhaps Epicurus is merely citing typical examples of intense pleasures under the heads of the four senses: (i.) taste; (ii.) touch; (iii.) hearing; (iv.) seeing. The omission of pleasant odours is curious; cf. Plato, *Phil.* 51 e θεῖον γένος ἡδονῶν.

that his bodily health was pitiful,[22] so much so that for many years he was unable to rise from his chair; and that he spent a whole mina daily on his table, as he himself says in his letter to Leontion and in that to the philosophers at Mitylene. Also that among other courtesans who consorted with him and Metrodorus were Mammarion and Hedia and Erotion and Nikidion. He alleges too that in his thirty-seven books *On Nature* Epicurus uses much repetition and writes largely in sheer opposition to others, especially to Nausiphanes, and here are his own words: "Nay, let them go hang: for, when labouring with an idea, he too had the sophist's off-hand boast-fulness like many another servile soul";

8. besides, he himself in his letters says of Nausiphanes: "This so maddened him that he abused me and called me pedagogue." Epicurus used to call this Nausiphanes jellyfish,[23] an illiterate, a fraud, and a trollop; Plato's school he called "the flatterers of Dionysius" [*Dionysokolakes*], their master himself the "golden" Plato,[24] and Aristotle a

---

[22] Cf. Aelian, Fr. 39 (*De Epicuro eiusque discipulis*). According to him the three brothers of Epicurus were all victims of disease. Plutarch (*Non posse suaviter*, etc., 1097 e) mentions the dropsy. However much his ailments were exaggerated by his enemies, they do not seem to have hindered him from literary work.

[23] Cf. Sext. Emp. *Adv. math.* i. 3 νῦν πλεύμονα καλῶν τὸν Ναυσιφάνην ὡς ἀναίσθητον; Plato, Phil. 21 c ζῆν δὲ οὐκ ἀνθρώπου βίον ἀλλά τινος πλεύμονος; Hesechius, s.v.; whence it appears that obtuseness and insensibility, not weakness or pliability, were the qualities imputed by this term.

[24] An ironical compliment, probably on Plato's style: cf. χρυσόστομος. It is not likely that Plato was ever regarded as a Midas or a golden simpleton, for which latter meaning Lucian, *Pro lapsu in sal*. i. ἐγὼ ὁ χρυσοῦς, is cited by Bignone.

profligate, who after devouring his patrimony took to soldiering and selling drugs; Protagoras a pack-carrier and the scribe of Democritus and village schoolmaster; Heraclitus a muddler;[25] Democritus Lerocritus (the nonsense-monger); and Antidorus Sannidorus (fawning gift-bearer); the Cynics foes of Greece; the Dialecticians despoilers; and Pyrrho an ignorant boor.

9. But these people are stark mad. For our philosopher has abundance of witnesses to attest his unsurpassed goodwill to all men — his native land, which honoured him with statues in bronze; his friends, so many in number that they could hardly be counted by whole cities, and indeed all who knew him, held fast as they were by the siren-charms of his doctrine, save Metrodorus[26] of Stratonicea, who went over to Carneades, being perhaps burdened by his master's excessive goodness; the School itself which, while nearly all the others have died out, continues for ever without interruption through numberless reigns of one scholarch after another;[27]

---

[25] In the same ironical sense in which Plato speaks of the Heracliteans who preached flux as τοὺς ῥέοντας (*Theaet*. 181 a), "themselves in flux."

[26] This man (not to be confounded with the more famous Metrodorus of Lampsacus, cf. 22) must belong to the second century B.C., if he was a contemporary of Carneades (c. 215-130 B.C.).

[27] So Aristocles; cf. Euseb. *Praep. Ev.* xiv. 21. 1, and Numenius, ib. xiv. 5. 3. The indications of time are so vague that this defence of Epicurus might be ascribed to D. L. himself. If, however, we compare the list of calumniators of Epicurus cited in 3, 4, we see that none of them is later than the Augustan age. To the same date belongs a passage in the article of *Suidas* on Epicurus – καὶ διέμεινεν ἡ αὐτοῦ σχόλη ἕως Καίσαρος τοῦ πρώτου ἔτη σκζ', ἐν οἷς διάδοχοι αὐτῆς ἐγένοντο ιδ'. As Usener has shown (*Epicurea*, 373), the interval of 227 years is reckoned from 270 to 44 B.C.

10. his gratitude to his parents, his generosity to his brothers, his gentleness to his servants, as evidenced by the terms of his will and by the fact that they were members of the School, the most eminent of them being the aforesaid Mys; and in general, his benevolence to all mankind. His piety towards the gods and his affection for his country no words can describe. He carried deference to others to such excess that he did not even enter public life. He spent all his life in Greece, notwithstanding the calamities which had befallen her in that age;[28] when he did once or twice take a trip to Ionia, it was to visit his friends there.[29] Friends indeed came to him from all parts and lived with him in his garden.

11. This is stated by Apollodorus, who also says that he purchased the garden for eighty minae; and to the same effect Diocles in the third book of his Epitome speaks of them as living a very simple and frugal life; at all events they were content with half a pint of thin wine and were, for the rest, thorough-going water-drinkers. He further says that Epicurus did not think it right that their property should be held in common, as required by the maxim of Pythagoras about the goods of friends; such a practice in his opinion implied mistrust, and without confidence there is no friendship. In his correspondence he himself mentions that he was content with plain bread and water. And again: "Send me a little pot of cheese,

---

[28] In the siege of Athens he is said to have maintained his disciples, counting out to each his ration of beans (Plut. *Demetr.* 34).
[29] Cf. *Epist.* 32 (Fr. 176 Usener). This celebrated letter to a child was written from Lampsacus on such a journey.

that, when I like, I may fare sumptuously." Such was the man who laid down that pleasure was the end of life. And here is the epigram[30] in which Athenaeus eulogizes him:

12.

> Ye toil, O men, for paltry things and incessantly begin strife and war for gain; but nature's wealth extends to a moderate bound, whereas vain judgements have a limitless range. This message Neocles' wise son heard from the Muses or from the sacred tripod at Delphi.[31]

And, as we go on, we shall know this better from his doctrines and his sayings.

Among the early philosophers, says Diocles, his favourite was Anaxagoras, although he occasionally disagreed with him, and Archelaus the teacher of Socrates. Diocles adds that he used to train his friends in committing his treatises to memory.[32]

13. Apollodorus in his *Chronology* tells us that our philosopher was a pupil of Nausiphanes and Praxiphanes;[33] but in his letter to Eurylochus, Epicurus himself denies it and says that he was self-taught. Both Epicurus and Hermarchus deny the very existence of Leucippus the philosopher, though by some and by Apollodorus the Epicurean he is said to have been the

---

[30] *Anth. Plan.* iv. 43.
[31] Cf. Petronius, *Sat.* 132.
[32] Cf. *infra*, 36, 83.
[33] If this Praxiphanes was the pupil of Theophrastus, considerations of age would make it highly improbable that he could have taught Epicurus; cf. Usener, Fr. 123.

teacher of Democritus. Demetrius the Magnesian affirms that Epicurus also attended the lectures of Xenocrates.

The terms he used for things were the ordinary terms, and Aristophanes the grammarian credits him with a very characteristic style. He was so lucid a writer that in the work *On Rhetoric* he makes clearness the sole requisite.

14. And in his correspondence he replaces the usual greeting, "I wish you joy," by wishes for welfare and right living, "May you do well," and "Live well."

Ariston[34] says in his *Life of Epicurus* that he derived his work entitled *The Canon* from the *Tripod* of Nausiphanes, adding that Epicurus had been a pupil of this man as well as of the Platonist Pamphilus[35] in Samos. Further, that he began to study philosophy when he was twelve years old, and started his own school at thirty-two.

He was born, according to Apollodorus in his *Chronology*, in the third year of the 109th Olympiad, in the archonship of Sosigenes[341 BCE], on the seventh day of the month Gamelion,[36] in the seventh year after the death of Plato.

---

[34] This is no doubt the Academic philosopher, Ariston of Alexandria, pupil of Antiochus, criticized by Philodemus in his Rhetoric, *V. H.*² iii. 168.
[35] Cf. *Suidas*, s.v.; Cic. *N. D.* i. 72.
[36] The eighth month of the Attic civil year. Thus he would be born about February, 341 B.C. Plato died 347 B.C.

15. When he was thirty-two he founded a school of philosophy, first in Mitylene and Lampsacus, and then five years later removed to Athens, where he died in the second year of the 127th Olympiad [271-270 BCE], in the archonship of Pytharatus, at the age of seventy-two; and Hermarchus the son of Agemortus, a Mitylenaean, took over the School. Epicurus died of renal calculus after an illness which lasted a fortnight: so Hermarchus tells us in his letters. Hermippus relates that he entered a bronze bath of lukewarm water and asked for unmixed wine, which he swallowed,

16. and then, having bidden his friends remember his doctrines, breathed his last.

Here is something of my own about him:[37]

Farewell, my friends; the truths I taught hold fast:
Thus Epicurus spake, and breathed his last.
He sat in a warm bath and neat wine quaff'd,
And straightway found chill death in that same draught.
Such was the life of the sage and such his end.

His last will was as follows: "On this wise I give and bequeath all my property to Amynomachus, son of Philocrates of Bate and Timocrates, son of Demetrius of Potamus, to each severally according to the items of the deed of gift laid up in the Metron,

17. on condition that they shall place the garden and all that pertains to it at the disposal of Hermarchus, son of Agemortus, of Mitylene, and the members of his society, and those whom Hermarchus may leave as his

---

[37] *Anth. Pal.* vii. 106.

successors, to live and study in.[38] And I entrust to my School in perpetuity the task of aiding Amynomachus and Timocrates and their heirs to preserve to the best of their power the common life in the garden in whatever way is best, and that these also (the heirs of the trustees) may help to maintain the garden in the same way as those to whom our successors in the School may bequeath it. And let Amynomachus and Timocrates permit Hermarchus and his fellow-members to live in the house in Melite for the lifetime of Hermarchus.

18. "And from the revenues made over by me to Amynomachus and Timocrates let them to the best of their power in consultation with Hermarchus make separate provision (1) for the funeral offerings to my father, mother, and brothers, and (2) for the customary celebration of my birthday on the tenth day of Gamelion in each year, and for the meeting of all my School held every month on the twentieth day to commemorate Metrodorus and myself according to the rules now in force.[39] Let them also join in celebrating the day in Poseideon which commemorates my brothers, and likewise the day in Metageitnion which commemorates Polyaenus, as I have done hitherto.

---

[38] Cf. v. 52 *supra*.
[39] That this custom lasted in the school for centuries is proved by the testimony of Cicero (*De fin*. ii. 101) and Pliny (*H. N.* xxxv. 5), as well as by the epigram of Philodemus (*Anth. Pal*. xi. 44). Cf. Athen. vii. 298 d; *supra*, vi. 101.

19. "And let Amynomachus and Timocrates take care of Epicurus, the son of Metrodorus, and of the son of Polyaenus, so long as they study and live with Hermarchus. Letthem likewise provide for the maintenance of Metrodorus's daughter,[40] so long as she is well-ordered and obedient to Hermarchus; and, when she comes of age, give her in marriage to a husband selected by Hermarchus from among the members of the School; and out of the revenues accruing to me let Amynomachus and Timocrates in consultation with Hermarchus give to them as much as they think proper for their maintenance year by year.

20. "Let them make Hermarchus trustee of the funds[41] along with themselves, in order that everything may be done in concert with him, who has grown old with me in philosophy and is left at the head of the School. And when the girl comes of age, let Amynomachus and Timocrates pay her dowry, taking from the property as much as circumstances allow, subject to the approval of Hermarchus. Let them provide for Nicanor as I have hitherto done, so that none of those members of the school who have rendered service to me in private life and have shown me kindness in every way and have chosen to grow old with me in the School should, so far as my means go, lack the necessaries of life.

---

[40] Possibly Dana: cf. Athen. xiii. 593 c.
[41] That funds were raised by friends of Epicurus and placed at his disposal is certain from the letter to Idomeneus: Plut. *Adv. Col.* 18, 1117 d (Usener fr. 130) πέμπε οὖν ἀπαρχὰς ἡμῖν εἰς τὴν τοῦ ἱεροῦ σώματος θεραπείαν. Nicanor seems to have been a recipient of this bounty. How like Auguste Comte!

21. "All my books to be given to Hermarchus.

"And if anything should happen to Hermarchus before the children of Metrodorus grow up, Amynomachus and Timocrates shall give from the funds bequeathed by me, so far as possible, enough for their several needs, as long as they are well ordered. And let them provide for the rest according to my arrangements; that everything may be carried out, so far as it lies in their power. Of my slaves I manumit Mys, Nicias, Lycon, and I also give Phaedrium her liberty."

22. And when near his end he wrote the following letter to Idomeneus:

"On this blissful day, which is also the last of my life, I write this to you. My continual sufferings from strangury and dysentery are so great that nothing could augment them; but over against them all I set gladness of mind at the remembrance of our past conversations. But I would have you, as becomes your life-long attitude to me and to philosophy, watch over the children of Metrodorus."

Such were the terms of his will.

Among his disciples, of whom there were many, the following were eminent: Metrodorus,[42] the son of Athenaeus (or of Timocrates) and of Sande, a citizen of Lampsacus, who from his first acquaintance with Epicurus never left him except once for six months spent on a visit to his native place, from which he returned to him again.

---

[42] Metrodorus (330-277 B.C.) was the master's beloved disciple; but the encomium preserved by Seneca (*Ep.* 52. 3) is certainly discriminating: "Epicurus says: 'quosdam indigere ope aliena, non ituros si nemo praecesserit, sed bene secuturos: ex his Metrodorum ait esse.'"

23. His goodness was proved in all ways, as Epicurus testifies in the introductions[43] to his works and in the third book of the Timocrates. Such he was: he gave his sister Batis to Idomeneus to wife, and himself took Leontion the Athenian courtesan as his concubine. He showed dauntless courage in meeting troubles and death, as Epicurus declares in the first book of his memoir. He died, we learn, seven years before Epicurus in his fifty-third year, and Epicurus himself in his will already cited clearly speaks of him as departed, and enjoins upon his executors to make provision for Metrodorus's children. The above-mentioned Timocrates[44] also, the brother of Metrodorus and a giddy fellow, was another of his pupils.

24. Metrodorus wrote the following works: *Against the Physicians*, in three books; *Of Sensations*; *Against Timocrates*; *Of Magnanimity*; *Of Epicurus's Weak Health*; *Against the Dialecticians*; *Against the Sophists*, in nine books; *The Way to Wisdom*; *Of Change*; *Of Wealth*; *In Criticism of Democritus*; *Of Noble Birth*.

Next came Polyaenus,[45] son of Athenodorus, a citizen of Lampsacus, a just and kindly man, as Philodemus and his

---

[43] Epicurus seems to have prefixed dedications or other short notices to the separate books of his larger works. Thus book xxviii. of his great work *On Nature* was dedicated to Hermarchus, and this has come down to us in *Vol. Herc. Coll. Alt.* vi. fr. 45 sqq.

[44] This second mention of Timocrates (see 6) may have been a marginal note, not very suitably placed, intended to distinguish the renegade Timocrates from his namesake, one of Epicurus' executors (18).

[45] One of the four pillars of the school: a great geometer until he became an Epicurean (Cic. *Ac. Pr.* 106 and *De fin.* i. 20). A letter of Epicurus to him is mentioned by Seneca (*Ep.* 18. 9).

pupils affirm. Next came Epicurus's successor Hermarchus, son of Agemortus, a citizen of Mytilene, the son of a poor man and at the outset a student of rhetoric.

There are in circulation the following excellent works by him:

25. *Correspondence concerning Empedocles*, in twenty-two books. *Of Mathematics*; *Against Plato*; *Against Aristotle*.

He died of paralysis, but not till he had given full proof of his ability.

And then there is Leonteus of Lampsacus and his wife Themista, to whom Epicurus wrote letters; further, Colotes[46] and Idomeneus, who were also natives of Lampsacus. All these were distinguished, and with them Polystra-tus, the successor of Hermarchus; he was succeeded by Dionysius, and he by Basilides. Apollodorus, known as the tyrant of the garden, who wrote over four hundred books, is also famous; and the two Ptolemaei of Alexandria, the one black and the other white; and Zeno[47] of Sidon, the pupil of Apollodorus, a voluminous author;

---

[46] Colotes, a great admirer of the master, wrote a work to prove that life is impossible by the rules of any other philosophy. Plutarch wrote a tract against him: Πρὸς Κολώτην, 1107e-1127; and also a rejoinder entitled, Οὐδὲ ζῆν ἔστιν ἡδέως κατ' Ἐπίκουρον, to prove that even a pleasurable life is unattainable on the principles of Epicurus.

[47] Cf. Cic. *Ac. Post.* 146; *N. D.* i. 59.

26. and Demetrius,[48] who was called the Laconian; and Diogenes of Tarsus, who compiled the select lectures; and Orion, and others whom the genuine Epicureans call Sophists.

There were three other men who bore the name of Epicurus: one the son of Leonteus and Themista; another a Magnesian by birth; and a third, a drill-sergeant.

Epicurus was a most prolific author and eclipsed all before him in the number of his writings: for they amount to about three hundred rolls, and contain not a single citation from other authors; it is Epicurus himself who speaks throughout. Chrysippus tried to outdo him in authorship according to Carneades, who therefore calls him the literary parasite of Epicurus. "For every subject treated by Epicurus, Chrysippus in his contentiousness must treat at equal length;

27. hence he has frequently repeated himself and set down the first thought that occurred to him, and in his haste has left things unrevised, and he has so many citations that they alone fill his books: nor is this unexampled in Zeno and Aristotle." Such, then, in number and character are the writings of Epicurus, the best of which are the following: *Of Nature*, thirty-seven books; *Of Atoms and Void*; *Of Love*; *Epitome of Objections to the Physicists*; *Against the Megarians*; *Problems*; *Sovran Maxims*; *Of Choice and Avoidance*; *Of*

---

[48] Cf. Sext. Emp. *Adv. math.* viii. 348 sqq.; Strabo, xiv. 658.

the End; *Of the Standard*, a work entitled *Canon*; *Chaeredemus*; *Of the Gods*; *Of Piety*;

28. *Hegesianax*; *Of Human Life*, four books; *Of Just Dealing*; *Neocles*: dedicated to Themista; *Symposium*; *Eurylochus*: dedicated to Metrodorus; *Of Vision*; *Of the Angle in the Atom*; *Of Touch*; *Of Fate*; *Theories of the Feelings* — against Timocrates; *Discovery of the Future*; *Introduction to Philosophy*; *Of Images*; *Of Presentation*; *Aristobulus*; *Of Music*; *Of Justice and the other Virtues*; *Of Benefits and Gratitude*; *Polymedes*; *Timocrates*, three books; *Metrodorus*, five books; *Antidorus*, two books; *Theories about Diseases (and Death)* — to Mithras[49]; *Callistolas*; *Of Kingship*; *Anaximenes*; *Correspondence*.

The views expressed in these works I will try to set forth by quoting three of his epistles, in which he has given an epitome of his whole system.

29. I will also set down his *Sovran Maxims* and any other utterance of his that seems worth citing, that you may be in a position to study the philosopher on all sides and know how to judge him.

The first epistle is addressed to Herodotus and deals with physics; the second to Pythocles and deals with astronomy or meteorology; the third is addressed to Menoeceus and its subject is human life. We must begin

---

[49] The full title, Περὶ νόσων καὶ θανάτου, "Of Diseases and Death," is preserved in a Herculaneum papyrus, 1012, col. 38, thus correcting our mss. of D. L.

with the first after some few preliminary remarks[50] upon his division of philosophy.

It is divided into three parts — Canonic, Physics, Ethics.

30. Canonic forms the introduction to the system and is contained in a single work entitled *The Canon*. The physical part includes the entire theory of Nature: it is contained in the thirty-seven books *Of Nature* and, in a summary form, in the letters. The ethical part deals with the facts of choice and aversion: this may be found in the books *On Human Life*, in the letters, and in his treatise *Of the End*. The usual arrangement, however, is to conjoin canonic with physics, and the former they call the science which deals with the standard and the first principle, or the elementary part of philosophy, while physics proper, they say, deals with becoming and perishing and with nature; ethics, on the other hand, deals with things to be sought and avoided, with human life and with the end-in-chief.

31. They reject dialectic as superfluous; holding that in their inquiries the physicists should be content to employ the ordinary terms for things.[51] Now in *The Canon* Epicurus affirms that our sensations and preconceptions and our feelings are the standards of truth; the Epicureans generally make perceptions of mental presentations[52] to be also standards. His own statements

---

[50] I.e., 29-34, the first of those summaries of doctrine which take up so much of Book X.
[51] An opinion often emphasized: e.g. 37, 73, 82, 152. Cf. Lucr. iii. 931 sqq.
[52] Such mental pictures are caused by atoms too fine to affect sense: cf. 64 *infra*; Lucr. ii. 740 sqq., iv. 722 sqq.; Cic. N. D. i. 54. On the whole

are also to be found in the *Summary* addressed to Herodotus and in the *Sovran Maxims*. Every sensation, he says, is devoid of reason and incapable of memory; for neither is it self-caused nor, regarded as having an external cause, can it add anything thereto or take anything therefrom.

32. Nor is there anything which can refute sensations or convict them of error: one sensation cannot convict another and kindred sensation, for they are equally valid; nor can one sensation refute another which is not kindred but heterogeneous, for the objects which the two senses judge are not the same;[53] nor again can reason refute them, for reason is wholly dependent on sensation; nor can one sense refute another, since we pay equal heed to all. And the reality of separate perceptions guarantees[54] the truth of our senses. But seeing and hearing are just as real as feeling pain. Hence it is from plain facts that we must start when we draw inferences about the unknown.[55] For all our notions are derived from perceptions, either by actual contact or by analogy, or resemblance, or composition, with some slight aid

---

subject consult Usener's *Epicurea*, Fr. 242-265, and, more especially, Sext. Emp. *Adv. math.* vii. 203-216.

[53] Cf. *inf.* 146.

[54] I.e., the trustworthiness of the senses [αἰσθήσεων] considered as faculties of sense-perception: cf. Sext. Emp. *Adv. math.* viii. 9 (Usener, Fr. 244).

[55] More precisely ἄδηλον = that which does not come within the range of sense. Compare e.g. 38 τὸ προσμένον καὶ τὸ ἄδηλον, and the way in which the conception of void is obtained in 40. In 62 it is called τὸ προσδοξαζόμενον περὶ τοῦ ἀοράτου.

from reasoning. And the objects presented to mad-men[56] and to people in dreams are true, for they produce effects — i.e. movements in the mind — which that which is unreal never does.

33. By preconception they mean a sort of apprehension or a right opinion or notion, or universal idea stored in the mind; that is, a recollection of an external object often presented, e.g. Such and such a thing is a man: for no sooner is the word "man" uttered than we think of his shape by an act of preconception, in which the senses take the lead.[57] Thus the object primarily denoted by every term is then plain and clear. And we should never have started an investigation, unless we had known what it was that we were in search of. For example: The object standing yonder is a horse or a cow. Before making this judgement, we must at some time or other have known by preconception the shape of a horse or a cow. We should not have given anything a name, if we had not first learnt its form by way of preconception. It follows, then, that preconceptions are clear. The object of a judgement is derived from something previously clear, by reference to which we frame the proposition, e.g. "How do we know that this is a man?" 34. Opinion they also call conception or assumption, and declare it to be true and false;[58] for it is true if it is subsequently confirmed or if it is not contradicted by evidence, and false if it is not subsequently confirmed or is contradicted

---

[56] Cf. Sext. Emp. *Adv. math.* viii. 63.
[57] I.e. in conformity with the sense-data which precede the recognition.
[58] See 124, where a true πρόληψις is opposed to a false ὑπόληψις. In Aristotle ὑπόληψις is often a synonym of δόξα · cf. Bonitz, *Index Ar.*, s.v.

by evidence. Hence the introduction of the phrase, "that which awaits" confirmation, e.g. to wait and get close to the tower and then learn what it looks like at close quarters.[59]

They affirm that there are two states of feeling, pleasure and pain, which arise in every animate being, and that the one is favourable and the other hostile to that being, and by their means choice and avoidance are determined;[60] and that there are two kinds of inquiry, the one concerned with things, the other with nothing but words.[61] So much, then, for his division[62] and criterion in their main outline.

But we must return to the letter.[63]

"Epicurus to Herodotus, greeting.

35.

> "For those who are unable to study carefully all my physical writings or to go into the longer treatises at all, I have myself prepared an epitome[64] of the whole system, Herodotus, to

---

[59] See 50, 147. The tower which seems round at a distance and square when we get up to it was the typical example in the school of that process of testing beliefs by observation which is here prescribed. Cf. Lucr. iv. 353 sqq., 501 sqq.; Sext. Emp. *Adv. math.* vii. 208.

[60] I.e., pleasure and pain are the criteria by which we choose and avoid.

[61] Cf. *inf.* 37.

[62] Division of philosophy is probably meant.

[63] The letter to Herodotus is the second and most valuable instalment of Epicurean doctrine. The manuscript seems to have been entrusted to a scribe to copy, just as it was: scholia and marginal notes, even where they interrupt the thread of the argument, have been faithfully reproduced. See 39, 40, 43, 44, 50, 66, 71, 73, 74, 75.

[64] This, as the most authentic summary of Epicurean physics which we possess, serves as a groundwork in modern histories, e.g. Zeller's. The

preserve in the memory enough of the principal doctrines,[65] to the end that on every occasion they may be able to aid themselves on the most important points, so far as they take up the study of Physics. Those who have made some advance in the survey of the entire system ought to fix in their minds under the principal headings an elementary outline of the whole treatment of the subject. For a comprehensive view is often required, the details but seldom.

36. "To the former, then — the main heads — we must continually return, and must memorize them so far as to get a valid conception of the facts, as well as the means of discovering all the details exactly when once the general outlines are rightly understood and remembered; since it is the privilege of the mature student to make a ready use of his conceptions by referring every one of them to elementary facts and simple terms. For it is impossible to gather up the results of continuous diligent study of the entirety of things, unless we can embrace in short formulas and hold in mind all that might have been accurately expressed even to the minutest detail.

37. "Hence, since such a course is of service to all who take up natural science, I, who devote to the subject my continuous energy and reap the calm enjoyment of a life like this, have prepared for you just such an epitome and manual of the doctrines as a whole.

"In the first place, Herodotus, you must understand what it is that words denote, in order that by reference to this we may be in a position to test opinions, inquiries, or problems, so that our proofs may not run on untested ad infinitum, nor the terms we use be empty of meaning.

---

reader may also consult with advantage Giussani, *Studi Lucreziani* (vol. i. of his Lucretius); Bignone, *Epicurea*, pp. 71-113; Hicks, *Stoic and Epicurean*, pp. 118-181.

[65] Only the principal doctrines are contained in this epistle; more, both general and particular, was given in the *Larger Compendium*.

38. For the primary signification of every term employed must be clearly seen, and ought to need no proving;[66] this being necessary, if we are to have something to which the point at issue or the problem or the opinion before us can be referred. "Next, we must by all means stick to our sensations, that is, simply to the present impressions whether of the mind or of any criterion whatever, and similarly to our actual feelings, in order that we may have the means of determining that which needs confirmation and that which is obscure.

"When this is clearly understood, it is time to consider generally things which are obscure. To begin with, nothing comes into being out of what is non-existent.[67] For in that case anything would have arisen out of anything, standing as it would in no need of its proper germs.[68]

39. And if that which disappears had been destroyed and become non-existent, everything would have perished, that into which the things were dissolved being non-existent. Moreover, the sum total of things was always such as it is now, and such it will ever remain. For there is nothing into which it can change. For outside the sum of things there is nothing which could enter into it and bring about the change.

"Further [*this he says also in the Larger Epitome near the beginning and in his First Book "On Nature"*], the whole of being consists of bodies and space.[69] For the existence of bodies is everywhere attested by sense itself, and it is upon

---

[66] Epicurus explains this more fully in Fr. 258 (Usener, p. 189). For „proof" and „proving" Bignone substitutes „declaration" and „declare."

[67] This is no innovation of Epicurus but a tenet common to all the pre-Socratics: the One, or Nature as a whole, assumed by the Ionians, is unchangeable in respect of generation and destruction; cf. Aristotle, *Met.* i. 3. 984 a 31. The pluralists were naturally even more explicit: see the well-known fragments, Anax. 17 d, Emped. 8 d. Lucretius (i. 180 f.) expands the doctrine.

[68] Cf. 41, 54. Lucr. i. 125 f. is the best commentary.

[69] Usener's insertion of "bodies and space" comes from 86; cf. Diels, *Dox. Gr.* 581. 28.

sensation that reason must rely when it attempts to infer the unknown from the known.

40. And if there were no space (which we call also void and place and intangible nature),[70] bodies would have nothing in which to be and through which to move, as they are plainly seen to move. Beyond bodies and space there is nothing which by mental apprehension or on its analogy we can conceive to exist. When we speak of bodies and space, both are regarded as wholes or separate things, not as the properties or accidents of separate things.

"Again [*he repeats this in the First Book and in Books XIV. and XV. of the work "On Nature" and in the Larger Epitome*], of bodies some are composite, others the elements of which these composite bodies are made.

41. These elements are indivisible and unchangeable, and necessarily so, if things are not all to be destroyed and pass into non-existence, but are to be strong enough to endure when the composite bodies are broken up, because they possess a solid nature and are incapable of being anywhere or anyhow dissolved.[71] It follows that the first beginnings must be indivisible, corporeal entities.

"Again, the sum of things is infinite. For what is finite has an extremity, and the extremity of anything is discerned only by comparison with something else. (Now the sum of things is not discerned by comparison with anything else:[72] hence, since it has no extremity, it has no limit; and, since it has no limit, it must be unlimited or infinite.

"Moreover, the sum of things is unlimited both by reason of the multitude of the atoms and the extent of the void.

42. For if the void were infinite and bodies finite, the bodies would not have stayed anywhere but would have been dispersed in their course through the infinite void, not having

---

[70] Cf. Lucr. i. 426.
[71] Cf. 54.
[72] The missing premiss is supplied by Cicero, *De div.* ii. 103 "at quod omne est, id non cernitur ex alio extrinsecus." Cf. Lucr. i. 960.

any supports or counter-checks to send them back on their upward rebound. Again, if the void were finite, the infinity of bodies would not have anywhere to be.

"Furthermore, the atoms, which have no void in them — out of which composite bodies arise and into which they are dissolved — vary indefinitely in their shapes; for so many varieties of things as we see could never have arisen out of a recurrence of a definite number of the same shapes. The like atoms of each shape are absolutely infinite; but the variety of shapes, though indefinitely large, is not absolutely infinite.

43. [*For neither does the divisibility go on "ad infinitum," he says below;*[73] *but he adds, since the qualities change, unless one is prepared to keep enlarging their magnitudes also simply "ad infinitum."*]

"The atoms are in continual motion through all eternity. [*Further, he says below, that the atoms move with equal speed, since the void makes way for the lightest and heaviest alike.*] Some of them rebound to a considerable distance from each other, while others merely oscillate in one place when they chance to have got entangled or to be enclosed by a mass of other atoms shaped for entangling.[74]

44. "This is because each atom is separated from the rest by void, which is incapable of offering any resistance to the rebound; while it is the solidity of the atom which makes it rebound after a collision, however short the distance to which it rebounds, when it finds itself imprisoned in a mass of entangling atoms. Of all this there is no beginning, since both

---

[73] Properly "further within" — a proof that the Scholiast read his Epicurus from a papyrus scroll which had to be unrolled. Hence "further within" or "nearer the centre" expresses the same thing as "further on" or "below" in a modern book.

[74] Note the distinction between (1) solids, composed of interlacing atoms (which have got entangled), and (2) fluids, composed of atoms not interlaced, needing a sheath or container of other atoms, if they are to remain united. To (2) belongs Soul (66). See Lucr. ii. 80-141; Cic. *De fin.* i. 7.

atoms and void exist from everlasting. [*He says below that atoms have no quality at all except shape, size, and weight. But that colour varies with the arrangement of the atoms he states in his "Twelve Rudiments"; further, that they are not of any and every size; at any rate no atom has ever been seen by our sense.*]

45. "The repetition at such length of all that we are now recalling to mind furnishes an adequate outline for our conception of the nature of things.

"Moreover, there is an infinite number of worlds, some like this world, others unlike it.[75] For the atoms being infinite in number, as has just been proved, are borne ever further in their course. For the atoms out of which a world might arise, or by which a world might be formed, have not all been expended on one world or a finite number of worlds, whether like or unlike this one. Hence there will be nothing to hinder an infinity of worlds.

46. "Again, there are outlines or films, which are of the same shape as solid bodies, but of a thinness far exceeding that of any object that we see. For it is not impossible that there should be found in the surrounding air combinations of this kind, materials adapted for expressing the hollowness and thinness of surfaces, and effluxes preserving the same relative position and motion which they had in the solid objects from which they come. To these films we give the name of 'images' or 'idols.' Furthermore, so long as nothing comes in the way to offer resistance, motion through the void accomplishes any imaginable distance in an inconceivably short time. For resistance encountered is the equivalent of slowness, its absence the equivalent of speed.

47. "Not that, if we consider the minute times perceptible by reason alone,[76] the moving body itself arrives at more than one

---

[75] This remark is not misplaced. For infinity of worlds follows from the infinity of (a) atoms, (b) space; see *inf.* 73, 89; Lucr. ii. 1048 foll.

[76] Cf. Lucr. iv. 794-8: "In one unit of time, when we can perceive it by sense and while one single word is uttered, many latent times are contained which reason finds to exist." Obviously such minute "times" are immeasurably

place simultaneously (for this too is inconceivable), although in time perceptible to sense it does arrive simultaneously, however different the point of departure from that conceived by us. For if it changed its direction, that would be equivalent to its meeting with resistance, even if up to that point we allow nothing to impede the rate of its flight. This is an elementary fact which in itself is well worth bearing in mind. In the next place the exceeding thinness of the images is contradicted by none of the facts under our observation. Hence also their velocities are enormous, since they always find a void passage to fit them. Besides, their incessant effluence meets with no resistance,[77] or very little, although many atoms, not to say an unlimited number, do at once encounter resistance.

48. "Besides this, remember that the production of the images is as quick as thought. For particles are continually streaming off from the surface of bodies, though no diminution of the bodies is observed, because other particles take their place.[78] And those given off for a long time retain the position and arrangement which their atoms had when they formed part of the solid bodies, although occa-sionally they are thrown into confusion. Sometimes such films[79] are formed very rapidly in the air, because they need not have any solid content; and there are other modes in which they may be formed. For there is nothing in all this which is contradicted by sensation, if we in some sort look at the clear evidence of sense, to which we

---

short. The unit of sensible time appears to be that called (in 62) "the minimum continuous time." Cf. Sext. Emp. x. 148-154.

[77] Or, inserting τὸ, not τῷ, before τῷ ἀπείρῳ, "a passage of the proper size to secure that nothing obstructs their endless emanation." But the meaning cannot be called certain.

[78] If vision is to be not merely intermittent but continuous, images must be perpetually streaming from the objects seen to our eyes; there must be a continual succession of similar images. Cf. Fr. 282 (Us.); Lucr. ii. 67-76, iv. 143-167.

[79] E.g. mirage and monstrous shapes of clouds: Lucr. iv. 129-142; Diod. iii. 56.

should also refer the continuity of particles in the objects external to ourselves.

49. "We must also consider that it is by the entrance of something coming from external objects that we see their shapes and think of them.[80] For external things would not stamp on us their own nature of colour and form through the medium of the air which is between them and us,[81] or by means of rays of light or currents of any sort going from us to them, so well as by the entrance into our eyes or minds, to whichever their size is suitable, of certain films coming from the things themselves, these films or outlines being of the same colour and shape as the external things themselves.

50. They move with rapid motion;[82] and this again explains why they present the appearance of the single continuous object, and retain the mutual interconnexion which they had in the object, when they impinge upon the sense, such impact being due to the oscillation of the atoms in the interior of the solid object from which they come. And whatever presentation we derive by direct contact, whether it be with the mind or with the sense-organs, be it shape that is presented or other properties, this shape as presented is the shape of the solid thing, and it is due either to a close coherence of the image as a whole or to a mere remnant of its parts. Falsehood and error always depend upon the intrusion of opinion[83] (when a fact awaits) confirmation or the absence of contradiction, which fact is afterwards frequently not confirmed (or even contradicted) [*following a certain movement in ourselves*

---

[80] Thought, as well as vision, is explained by images, but images of a much finer texture, which fail to affect the eyes but do affect the mind: cf. Fr. 317 (Us.); Lucr. iv. 777 f.

[81] This was the view of Democritus; cf. Beare, *Greek Theories of Elementary Cognition*, p. 26.

[82] The reader is left to infer that, the more rapid the motion, the more continuous is the succession of fresh images. It is this uninterrupted train of images which guarantees the continued existence of the external object, just as their similarity or identity guarantees its oneness: cf. Lucr. iv. 87, 104 f., 189, 256 f., 714 f.; Cic. N. D. i. 105.

[83] Cf. Fr. 247-254 (Us.); Lucr. iv. 462-468, 723-826.

Life of Epicurus

connected with, but distinct from, the mental picture presented — which is the cause of error.]

51. "For the presentations which, e.g., are received in a picture or arise in dreams, or from any other form of apprehension by the mind or by the other criteria of truth, would never have resembled what we call the real and true things, had it not been for certain actual things of the kind with which we come in contact. Error would not have occurred, if we had not experienced some other movement in ourselves, conjoined with, but distinct from,[84] the perception of what is presented. And from this movement, if it be not confirmed or be contradicted, falsehood results; while, if it be confirmed or not contradicted, truth results.

52. "And to this view we must closely adhere, if we are not to repudiate the criteria founded on the clear evidence of sense, nor again to throw all these things into confusion by maintaining falsehood as if it were truth.[85]

"Again, hearing takes place when a current passes from the object, whether person or thing, which emits voice or sound or noise, or produces the sensation of hearing in any way whatever. This current is broken up into homogeneous particles, which at the same time preserve a certain mutual connexion and a distinctive unity extending to the object which emitted them, and thus, for the most part, cause the perception in that case or, if not, merely indicate the presence of the external object.

53. For without the transmission from the object of a certain interconnexion of the parts no such sensation could arise. Therefore we must not suppose that the air itself is moulded into shape by the voice emitted or something similar;[86] for it is

---

[84] διάληψιν ἔχειν, "to be distinct"; again, 58; so διαληπτόν, "distinguishable" (57).

[85] Epicurus was a severe critic of the Sceptics; cf. 146, 147; Frs. 252, 254 (Us.); Lucr. iv. 507-521.

[86] Air is not, as Democritus held (Beare, op. cit. p. 99), the medium, any more than for vision (49). By "something similar" Epicurus probably means

very far from being the case that the air is acted upon by it in this way. The blow which is struck in us when we utter a sound causes such a displacement of the particles as serves to produce a current resembling breath, and this displacement gives rise to the sensation of hearing.

"Again, we must believe that smelling,[87] like hearing, would produce no sensation, were there not particles conveyed from the object which are of the proper sort for exciting the organ of smelling, some of one sort, some of another, some exciting it confusedly and strangely, others quietly and agreeably.

54. "Moreover, we must hold that the atoms in fact possess none of the qualities belonging to things which come under our observation, except shape, weight, and size, and the properties necessarily conjoined with shape.[88] For every quality changes, but the atoms do not change, since, when the composite bodies are dissolved, there must needs be a permanent something, solid and indissoluble, left behind, which makes change possible: not changes into or from the non-existent, but often through differences of arrangement, and sometimes through additions and subtractions of the atoms.[89] Hence these somethings capable of being diversely arranged must be indestructible, exempt from change, but

---

to include sound or noise. Lucretius treats of hearing in iv. 524-614, ii. 410-413.

[87] Cf. Lucr. iv. 673-705, ii. 414-417. Neither taste nor touch is treated separately in this epistle.

[88] For shape cf. Lucr. ii. 333-521, iii. 185-202; for weight cf. Lucr. ii. 184-215, i. 358-367. For qualities generally cf. Epic. Frs. 288, 289 (Us.); Sext. Emp. *Adv. math.* ix. 335. Atoms have no colour (Frs. 29, 30, 289; Lucr. ii. 730-841), nor smell (Lucr. ii. 846-855) nor flavour nor sound nor cold nor heat (ib. 856-859), in short no variable quality (ib. 859-864); but the various qualities are due to the arrangement, positions, motions, and shape of the component atoms.

[89] If something unchanging underlies every change, the transformation of things and of their qualities must be due to the motion of the component atoms. With ἐν πολλοῖς understand στερεμνίοις: the arrangement of the atoms varies in solid objects.

possessed each of its own distinctive mass[90] and configuration. This must remain.

55. "For in the case of changes of configuration within our experience the figure is supposed to be inherent when other qualities are stripped off, but the qualities are not supposed, like the shape which is left behind, to inhere in the subject of change, but to vanish altogether from the body. Thus, then, what is left behind is sufficient to account for the differences in composite bodies, since something at least must necessarily be left remaining and be immune from annihilation.

"Again, you should not suppose that the atoms have any and every size,[91] lest you be contradicted by facts; but differences of size must be admitted; for this addition renders the facts of feeling and sensation easier of explanation.

56. But to attribute any and every magnitude to the atoms does not help to explain the differences of quality in things; moreover, in that case atoms large enough to be seen ought to have reached us, which is never observed to occur; nor can we conceive how its occurrence should be possible, i.e. that an atom should become visible.[92]

"Besides, you must not suppose that there are parts unlimited in number, be they ever so small, in any finite body. Hence not only must we reject as impossible sub-division *ad infinitum* into smaller and smaller parts, lest we make all things too weak and, in our conceptions of the aggregates, be driven to pulverize the things that exist, i.e. the atoms, and annihilate[93]

---

[90] In 53 ὄγκος was translated "particle," since the context shows that a group of atoms analogous to a visible film is meant. But here each of the permanent somethings, i.e. the atoms, has its own mass [ὄγκος] and configuration.

[91] The opinion of Democritus.

[92] Cf. Lucr. iv. 110-128, i. 599-627, ii. 478-521. The first of these passages states that the atom is "far below the ken of our senses" and "much smaller than the things which our eyes begin to be able to see."

[93] Admitting indivisible atoms, hard solid bodies can be explained; whereas, if atoms were soft and thus divisible *ad infinitum*, all things would be

them; but in dealing with finite things we must also reject as impossible the progression *ad infinitum* by less and less increments.

57. "For when once we have said that an infinite number of particles, however small, are contained in anything, it is not possible to conceive how it could any longer be limited or finite in size. For clearly our infinite number of particles must have some size; and then, of whatever size they were, the aggregate they made would be infinite. And, in the next place, since what is finite has an extremity which is distinguishable, even if it is not by itself observable, it is not possible to avoid thinking of another such extremity next to this. Nor can we help thinking that in this way, by proceeding forward from one to the next in order, it is possible by such a progression to arrive in thought at infinity.[94]

58. "We must consider the minimum perceptible by sense as not corresponding to that which is capable of being traversed, i.e. is extended,[95] nor again as utterly unlike it, but as having something in common with the things capable of being traversed, though it is without distinction of parts. But when from the illusion created by this common property we think we shall distinguish something in the minimum, one part on one side and another part on the other side, it must be another minimum equal to the first which catches our eye. In fact, we see these minima one after another, beginning with the first,

---

deprived of solidity (Lucr. i. 565-576). Just before Lucretius has argued that, if atoms did not set a limit to the division of things, production or reproduction would be impossible, since destruction is wrought more quickly than it is repaired, and endless future time could not undo the waste of endless past time. Possibly, however, Epicurus is thinking of an argument similar to that used by Lucretius in ii. 522-568 — that a finite number of shapes implies and requires an infinity of atoms of each shape.

[94] Each visible body is the sum of minima, or least perceptible points, which, because they are of finite size, are also finite in number.

[95] "That which admits the successive transitions from part to part." As Bignone remarks, a mathematical series, whether of integers or fractions or powers, might be so described. But Epicurus is obviously dealing with areas and surfaces; since generally to us the "visible" will also be extended.

and not as occupying the same space; nor do we see them touch one another's parts with their parts, but we see that by virtue of their own peculiar character (i.e., as being unit indivisibles) they afford a means of measuring magnitudes: there are more of them, if the magnitude measured is greater; fewer of them, if the magnitude measured is less.

"We must recognize that this analogy also holds of the minimum in the atom;

59. it is only in minuteness that it differs from that which is observed by sense, but it follows the same analogy. On the analogy of things within our experience we have declared that the atom has magnitude; and this, small as it is, we have merely reproduced on a larger scale. And further, the least and simplest[96] things must be regarded as extremities of lengths, furnishing from themselves as units the means of measuring lengths, whether greater or less, the mental vision being employed, since direct observation is impossible. For the community which exists between them and the unchangeable parts (i.e. the minimal parts of area or surface) is sufficient to justify the conclusion so far as this goes. But it is not possible that these minima of the atom should group themselves together through the possession of motion.[97]

60. "Further, we must not assert 'up' or 'down' of that which is unlimited, as if there were a zenith or nadir.[98] As to the space overhead, however, if it be possible to draw[99] a line to infinity from the point where we stand, we know that never will this space — or, for that matter, the space below the supposed

---

[96] I.e. "uncompounded." But v. Arnim's ἀμεῆ, "void of parts," is more suitable.

[97] The parts of the atom are incapable of motion; cf. Lucr. i. 628-634.

[98] Objection was taken by Aristotle to the atomic motion of Democritus, on the ground that it implied a point or region absolutely high, and an opposite point or region absolutely low, these terms being unmeaning in infinite space (Aristotle, *Phys.* iii. 5. 205 b 30; iv. 8. 215 a 8). See *Classical Review*, xxxv. p. 108.

[99] This verb [ἄγειν] is technical in Euclid.

standpoint if produced to infinity — appear to us to be at the same time 'up' and 'down' with reference to the same point; for this is inconceivable. Hence it is possible to assume one direction of motion, which we conceive as extending upwards *ad infinitum*, and another downwards, even if it should happen ten thousand times that what moves from us to the spaces above our heads reaches the feet of those above us, or that which moves downwards from us the heads of those below us. None the less is it true that the whole of the motion in the respective cases is conceived as extending in opposite directions *ad infinitum*.

61. "When they are travelling through the void and meet with no resistance, the atoms must move with equal speed. Neither will heavy atoms travel more quickly than small and light ones, so long as nothing meets them, nor will small atoms travel more quickly than large ones, provided they always find a passage suitable to their size, and provided also that they meet with no obstruction. Nor will their upward or their lateral motion, which is due to collisions, nor again their downward motion, due to weight, affect their velocity. As long as either motion obtains, it must continue, quick as the speed of thought, provided there is no obstruction, whether due to external collision or to the atoms' own weight counteracting the force of the blow.

62. "Moreover, when we come to deal with composite bodies, one of them will travel faster than another, although their atoms have equal speed. This is because the atoms in the aggregates are travelling in one direction[100] during the shortest continuous time, albeit they move in different directions in times so short as to be appreciable only by the reason, but frequently collide until the continuity of their motion is appreciated by sense. For the assumption that beyond the range of direct observation even the minute times conceivable

---

[100] When the atoms in a composite body are, during a continuous sensible time, however short, all moving in one single direction, then the composite body will be travelling from place to place and have a relative velocity.

by reason will present continuity of motion is not true in the case before us. Our canon is that direct observation by sense and direct apprehension by the mind are alone invariably true. 63. "Next, keeping in view our perceptions and feelings (for so shall we have the surest grounds for belief), we must recognize generally that the soul is a corporeal thing, composed of fine particles, dispersed all over the frame,[101] most nearly resembling wind with an admixture of heat,[102] in some respects like wind, in others like heat. But, again, there is the third part which exceeds the other two in the fineness of its particles and thereby keeps in closer touch with the rest of the frame.[103] And this is shown by the mental faculties and feelings, by the ease with which the mind moves, and by thoughts, and by all those things the loss of which causes death. 64. Further, we must keep in mind that soul has the greatest share in causing sensation. Still, it would not have had sensation, had it not been somehow confined within the rest of the frame. But the rest of the frame, though it provides this indispensable condition[104] for the soul, itself also has a share, derived from the soul, of the said quality; and yet does not possess all the qualities of soul. Hence on the departure of the soul it loses sentience. For it had not this power in itself; but something else, congenital with the body, supplied it to body: which other thing, through the potentiality actualized in it by means of motion, at once acquired for itself a quality of sentience, and, in virtue of the neighbourhood and

---

[101] Cf. Lucr. iii. 161-176, 177-230.
[102] Cf. Lucr. iii. 231-257, 425-430; Epic. Fr. (Us.) 315, 314. These authorities assume *four* component elements, while in this epistle one of these [ἀερῶδές τι] is omitted.
[103] The so-called "nameless" substance [*nominis expers* Lucr. iii. 242, ἀκατονόμαστον in Epicurus].
[104] The body, by keeping soul-atoms together without much dispersion, allows them to vibrate with the motions that generate sentience and sensation.

Diogenes Laërtius

interconnexion between them, imparted it (as I said) to the body also.

65. "Hence, so long as the soul is in the body, it never loses sentience through the removal of some other part. The containing sheath[105] may be dislocated in whole or in part, and portions of the soul may thereby be lost; yet in spite of this the soul, if it manage to survive, will have sentience. But the rest of the frame, whether the whole of it survives or only a part, no longer has sensation, when once those atoms have departed, which, however few in number, are required to constitute the nature of soul. Moreover, when the whole frame is broken up,[106] the soul is scattered and has no longer the same powers as before, nor the same motions; hence it does not possess sentience either.

66. "For we cannot think of it[107] as sentient, except it be in this composite whole and moving with these movements; nor can we so think of it when the sheaths which enclose and surround it are not the same as those in which the soul is now located and in which it performs these movements. [*He says elsewhere that the soul is composed of the smoothest and roundest of atoms, far superior in both respects to those of fire; that part of it is irrational, this being scattered over the rest of the frame, while the rational part resides in the chest, as is manifest from our fears and our joy; that sleep occurs when the parts of the soul which have been scattered all over the composite organism are held fast in it or dispersed, and afterwards collide with one another by their impacts. The semen is derived from the whole of the body.*]

---

[105] Since the participle στεγάζον is also found in the plural [στεγάζοντα], it seems best to assume with Bignone that the whole frame is regarded as the sum of parts, each of which serves as the envelope, sheath, or container of some part of the soul. Thus the loss of a limb is not fatal to life, because the rest of the frame has served in its capacity of envelope to preserve a sufficient number of soul-atoms in working order.

[106] Cf. Lucr. ii. 944-962.

[107] It = the soul, the logical subject, the neuter replacing the more appropriate feminine pronoun.

67. "There is the further point to be considered, what the incorporeal can be, if, I mean, according to current usage the term is applied to what can be conceived as self-existent.[108] But it is impossible to conceive anything that is incorporeal as self-existent except empty space. And empty space cannot itself either act or be acted upon, but simply allows body to move through it. Hence those who call soul incorporeal speak foolishly. For if it were so, it could neither act nor be acted upon. But, as it is, both these properties, you see, plainly belong to soul.

68. "If, then, we bring all these arguments concerning soul to the criterion of our feelings and perceptions, and if we keep in mind the proposition stated at the outset, we shall see that the subject has been adequately comprehended in outline: which will enable us to determine the details with accuracy and confidence.

"Moreover, shapes and colours, magnitudes and weights, and in short all those qualities which are predicated of body, in so far as they are perpetual properties either of all bodies or of visible bodies, are knowable by sensation of these very properties: these, I say, must not be supposed to exist independently by themselves[109] (for that is inconceivable),

69. nor yet to be non-existent, nor to be some other and incorporeal entities cleaving to body,[110] nor again to be parts of body. We must consider the whole body in a general way to derive its permanent nature from all of them, though it is not, as it were, formed by grouping them together in the same way as when from the particles themselves a larger aggregate is made up, whether these particles be primary or any magnitudes whatsoever less than the particular whole. All

---

[108] Or, if ὅτι τὸ ἀσώματον λέγομεν be read, "that according to current usage we apply the term *incorporeal* to that which can be conceived as self-existent."

[109] Cf. Lucr. i. 449 f.; Sext. Emp. *Adv. math.* x. 221-223.

[110] Cf. Lucr. i. 478-482.

these qualities, I repeat, merely give the body its own permanent nature. They all have their own characteristic modes of being perceived and distinguished, but always along with the whole body in which they inhere and never in separation from it; and it is in virtue of this complete conception of the body as a whole that it is so designated.

70. "Again, qualities often attach to bodies without being permanent concomitants. They are not to be classed among invisible entities nor are they incorporeal. Hence, using the term 'accidents'[111] in the commonest sense, we say plainly that 'accidents' have not the nature of the whole thing to which they belong, and to which, conceiving it as a whole, we give the name of body, nor that of the permanent properties without which body cannot be thought of. And in virtue of certain peculiar modes of apprehension into which the complete body always enters, each of them can be called an accident.

71. But only as often as they are seen actually to belong to it, since such accidents are not perpetual concomitants. There is no need to banish from reality this clear evidence that the accident has not the nature of that whole — by us called body — to which it belongs, nor of the permanent properties which accompany the whole. Nor, on the other hand, must we suppose the accident to have independent existence (for this is just as inconceivable in the case of accidents as in that of the permanent properties); but, as is manifest, they should all be regarded as accidents, not as permanent concomitants, of bodies, nor yet as having the rank of independent existence. Rather they are seen to be exactly as and what sensation itself makes them individually claim to be.

72. "There is another thing which we must consider carefully. We must not investigate time as we do the other accidents which we investigate in a subject, namely, by referring them to the preconceptions envisaged in our minds; but we must take into account the plain fact itself, in virtue of which we speak

---

[111] Cf. Lucr. i. 455 f., where slavery, poverty, riches, war and peace are the examples chosen, as elsewhere are rest and motion.

of time as long or short, linking to it in intimate connexion this attribute of duration.[112] We need not adopt any fresh terms as preferable, but should employ the usual expressions about it. Nor need we predicate anything else of time, as if this something else contained the same essence as is contained in the proper meaning of the word 'time' (for this also is done by some). We must chiefly reflect upon that to which we attach this peculiar character of time, and by which we measure it.

73. No further proof is required: we have only to reflect that we attach the attribute of time to days and nights and their parts, and likewise to feelings of pleasure and pain and to neutral states, to states of movement and states of rest, conceiving a peculiar accident of these to be this very characteristic which we express by the word 'time.' [*He says this both in the second book "On Nature" and in the Larger Epitome.*]

"After the foregoing we have next to consider that the worlds and every finite aggregate which bears a strong resemblance to things we commonly see have arisen out of the infinite.[113] For all these, whether small or great, have been separated off from special conglomerations of atoms; and all things are again dissolved,[114] some faster, some slower, some through the action of one set of causes, others through the action of another. [*It is clear, then, that he also makes the worlds perishable, as their parts are subject to change. Elsewhere he says the earth is supported on the air.*]

74. "And further, we must not suppose that the worlds have necessarily one and the same shape. [*On the contrary, in the twelfth book "On Nature" he himself says that the shapes of the worlds differ, some being spherical, some oval, others again of shapes different from these. They do not, however, admit of every shape. Nor are they living beings which have been*

---

[112] Cf. Sext. Emp. *Adv. math.* x. 219 f., 224 f., 240-244.
[113] Cf. Lucr. ii. 1048-1089.
[114] Cf. Lucr. ii. 1144, 1145; Stob. *Ecl.* i. 20, 172 W.

separated from the infinite.] For nobody can prove that in one sort of world there might not be contained, whereas in another sort of world there could not possibly be, the seeds out of which animals and plants arise and all the rest of the things we see. [*And the same holds good for their nurture in a world after they have arisen. And so too we must think it happens upon the earth also.*]

75. "Again, we must suppose that nature[115] too has been taught and forced to learn many various lessons by the facts themselves, that reason subsequently develops what it has thus received and makes fresh discoveries, among some tribes more quickly, among others more slowly, the progress thus made being at certain times and seasons greater, at others less.

"Hence even the names of things were not originally due to convention,[116] but in the several tribes under the impulse of special feelings and special presentations of sense primitive man uttered special cries.[117] The air thus emitted was moulded by their individual feelings or sense-presentations, and differently according to the difference of the regions which the tribes inhabited.

76. Subsequently whole tribes adopted their own special names, in order that their communications might be less ambiguous to each other and more briefly expressed. And as for things not visible, so far as those who were conscious of them tried to introduce any such notion, they put in circulation certain names for them, either sounds which they were instinct-ively compelled to utter or which they selected by reason on analogy according to the most general cause there can be for expressing oneself in such a way.

"Nay more: we are bound to believe that in the sky revolutions, solstices, eclipses, risings and settings, and the like, take place without the ministration or command, either

---

[115] That is, nature working in primitive man, almost the same thing as instinct.
[116] Cf. Lucr. v. 1041 f. Heraclitus, Democritus, and Aristotle derived language from convention.
[117] CfSee Bignone, p. 107 note 3.. Lucr. v. 1028, 1029, 1056-1058.

now or in the future, of any being who at the same time enjoys perfect bliss along with immortality.

77. For troubles and anxieties and feelings of anger and partiality do not accord with bliss, but always imply weakness and fear and dependence upon one's neighbours. Nor, again, must we hold that things which are no more than globular masses of fire, being at the same time endowed with bliss, assume these motions at will. Nay, in every term we use we must hold fast to all the majesty which attaches to such notions as bliss and immortality, lest the terms should generate opinions inconsistent with this majesty. Otherwise such inconsistency will of itself suffice to produce the worst disturbance in our minds. Hence, where we find phenomena invariably recurring, the invariableness of the recurrence must be ascribed to the original interception and conglomeration of atoms whereby the world was formed.

78. "Further, we must hold that to arrive at accurate knowledge of the cause of things of most moment is the business of natural science, and that happiness depends on this (viz. on the knowledge of celestial and atmospheric phenomena), and upon knowing what the heavenly bodies really are, and any kindred facts contributing to exact knowledge in this respect.[118]

"Further, we must recognize on such points as this no plurality of causes or contingency, but must hold that nothing suggestive of conflict or disquiet is compatible with an immortal and blessed nature. And the mind can grasp the absolute truth of this.

79. "But when we come to subjects for special inquiry, there is nothing in the knowledge of risings and settings and solstices and eclipses and all kindred subjects that contributes to our happiness; but those who are well-informed about such matters and yet are ignorant what the heavenly bodies really are, and what are the most important causes of phenomena,

---

[118] I.e. to secure the end of happiness.

feel quite as much fear as those who have no such special information — nay, perhaps even greater fear, when the curiosity excited by this additional knowledge cannot find a solution or understand the subordination of these phenomena to the highest causes.

"Hence, if we discover more than one cause that may account for solstices, settings and risings, eclipses and the like, as we did also in particular matters of detail,

80. we must not suppose that our treatment of these matters fails of accuracy, so far as it is needful to ensure our tranquillity and happiness. When, therefore, we investigate the causes of celestial and atmospheric phenomena, as of all that is unknown, we must take into account the variety of ways in which analogous occurrences happen within our experience; while as for those who do not recognize the difference between what is or comes about from a single cause and that which may be the effect of any one of several causes, overlooking the fact that the objects are only seen at a distance, and are moreover ignorant of the conditions that render, or do not render, peace of mind impossible — all such persons we must treat with contempt. If then we think that an event could happen in one or other particular way out of several, we shall be as tranquil when we recognize that it actually comes about in more ways than one as if we knew that it happens in this particular way.

81. "There is yet one more point to seize, namely, that the greatest anxiety of the human mind arises through the belief that the heavenly bodies are blessed and indestructible, and that at the same time they have volitions and actions and causality inconsistent with this belief; and through expecting or apprehending some everlasting evil, either because of the myths, or because we are in dread of the mere insensibility of death, as if it had to do with us; and through being reduced to this state not by conviction but by a certain irrational perversity, so that, if men do not set bounds to their terror, they endure as much or even more intense anxiety than the man whose views on these matters are quite vague.

82. But mental tranquillity means being released from all these troubles and cherishing a continual remembrance of the highest and most important truths.

"Hence we must attend to present feelings and sense perceptions, whether those of mankind in general or those peculiar to the individual, and also attend to all the clear evidence available, as given by each of the standards of truth. For by studying them we shall rightly trace to its cause and banish the source of disturbance and dread, accounting for celestial phenomena and for all other things which from time to time befall us and cause the utmost alarm to the rest of mankind.

"Here then, Herodotus, you have the chief doctrines of Physics in the form of a summary.

83. So that, if this statement be accurately retained and take effect, a man will, I make no doubt, be incomparably better equipped than his fellows, even if he should never go into all the exact details. For he will clear up for himself many of the points which I have worked out in detail in my complete exposition; and the summary itself, if borne in mind, will be of constant service to him.

"It is of such a sort that those who are already tolerably, or even perfectly, well acquainted with the details can, by analysis of what they know into such elementary perceptions as these, best prosecute their researches in physical science as a whole; while those, on the other hand, who are not altogether entitled to rank as mature students can in silent fashion and as quick as thought run over the doctrines most important for their peace of mind."

Such is his epistle on *Physics*. Next comes the epistle on *Celestial Phenomena*.

"Epicurus to Pythocles, greeting.

84.

"In your letter to me, of which Cleon was the bearer, you continue to show me affection which I have merited by my devotion to you, and you try, not without success, to recall the considerations which make for a happy life. To aid your memory you ask me for a clear and concise statement respecting celestial phenomena; for what we have written on this subject elsewhere is, you tell me, hard to remember, although you have my books constantly with you. I was glad to receive your request and am full of pleasant expectations.

85. We will then complete our writing and grant all you ask. Many others besides you will find these reasonings useful, and especially those who have but recently made acquaintance with the true story of nature and those who are attached to pursuits which go deeper than any part of ordinary education. So you will do well to take and learn them and get them up quickly along with the short epitome in my letter to Herodotus.[119]

"In the first place, remember that, like everything else, knowledge of celestial phenomena, whether taken along with other things or in isolation, has no other end in view than peace of mind and firm conviction.[120]

86. We do not seek to wrest by force what is impossible, nor to understand all matters equally well, nor make our treatment always as clear as when we discuss human life or explain the principles of physics in general — for instance, that the whole of being consists of bodies and intangible nature, or that the ultimate elements of things are indivisible, or any other proposition which admits only one explanation of the phenomena to be possible. But this is not the case with celestial phenomena: these at any rate admit of manifold causes for their occurrence and manifold accounts, none of them contradictory of sensation, of their nature.

---

[119] This would seem decisive of what the *Shorter Catechism* of Epicurus really was; see, however, 135.

[120] Philosophy is defined as "an activity which by words and arguments secures the happy life" (Sext. Emp. *Adv. math.* xi. 169; cf. Epic. *Frag.* 222 Us.).

"For in the study of nature we must not conform to empty assumptions and arbitrary laws, but follow the promptings of the facts;
87. for our life has no need now of unreason and false opinion; our one need is untroubled existence. All things go on uninterruptedly, if all be explained by the method of plurality of causes in conformity with the facts, so soon as we duly understand what may be plausibly alleged respecting them. But when we pick and choose among them, rejecting one equally consistent with the phenomena, we clearly fall away from the study of nature altogether and tumble into myth. Some phenomena within our experience afford evidence by which we may interpret what goes on in the heavens. We see how the former really take place, but not how the celestial phenomena take place, for their occurrence may possibly be due to a variety of causes.
88. However, we must observe each fact as presented, and further separate from it all the facts presented along with it, the occurrence of which from various causes is not contradicted by facts within our experience.
"A world is a circumscribed portion of the universe, which contains stars and earth and all other visible things, cut off from the infinite, and terminating [*and terminating in a boundary which may be either thick or thin, a boundary whose dissolution will bring about the wreck of all within it*] in an exterior which may either revolve or be at rest, and be round or triangular or of any other shape whatever. All these alternatives are possible: they are contradicted by none of the facts in this world, in which an extremity can nowhere be discerned.
89. "That there is an infinite number of such worlds can be perceived, and that such a world may arise in a world or in one of the *intermundia* (by which term we mean the spaces between worlds) in a tolerably empty space and not, as some maintain, in a vast space perfectly clear and void.[121] It arises when certain suitable seeds rush in from a single world or

---

[121] Cf. Lucr. i. 334 ("locus intactus inane uacansque"), and ix. 31 *supra* for the view of Leucippus here rejected.

intermundium, or from several, and undergo gradual additions or articulations or changes of place, it may be, and waterings from appropriate sources, until they are matured and firmly settled in so far as the foundations laid can receive them.

90. For it is not enough that there should be an aggregation or a vortex in the empty space in which a world may arise, as the necessitarians hold, and may grow until it collide with another, as one of the so-called physicists[122] says. For this is in conflict with facts.

"The sun and moon and the stars generally were not of independent origin and later absorbed within our world, [such parts of it at least as serve at all for its defence]; but they at once began to take form and grow [and so too did earth and sea][123] by the accretions and whirling motions of certain substances of finest texture, of the nature either of wind or fire, or of both; for thus sense itself suggests.

91. "The size of the sun and the remaining stars relatively to us is just as great as it appears.[124] [*This he states in the eleventh book "On Nature." For, says he, if it had diminished in size on account of the distance, it would much more have diminished its brightness; for indeed there is no distance more proportionate to this diminution of size than is the distance at which the brightness begins to diminish.*] But in itself and actually it may be a little larger or a little smaller, or precisely as great as it is seen to be. For so too fires of which we have experience are seen by sense when we see them at a distance. And every objection brought against this part of the theory will easily be met by anyone who attends to plain facts, as I show in my work *On Nature*.

92. And the rising and setting of the sun, moon, and stars may be due to kindling and quenching,[125] provided that the

---

[122] Democritus; cf. Hippol. p. 565, 13 D φθείρεσθαι δὲ τοὺς κόσμους ὑπ' ἀλλήλων προσπίπτοντας; Atius ii. 4. 9.

[123] This must be a gloss, because earth and sea are made of less subtle atoms than the heavenly bodies.

[124] Cf. Lucr. v. 564-591; Philodemus Περὶ σημείων 10. 35 – 11. 8; Cic. *Acad. Pr.* 82, 123; De *Fin.* i. 20.

[125] The opinion of Heraclitus (p. 32 B, 6 D) and Xenophanes, and Metrodorus of Chios. Servius, however (ad Verg. G. i. 249, Aen. iv. 584), attributes the theory to the Epicureans.

circumstances are such as to produce this result in each of the two regions, east and west: for no fact testifies against this. Or the result might be produced by their coming forward above the earth and again by its intervention to hide them: for no fact testifies against this either. And their motions[126] may be due to the rotation of the whole heaven, or the heaven may be at rest and they alone rotate according to some necessary impulse to rise, implanted at first when the world was made

93. ... and this through excessive heat, due to a certain extension of the fire which always encroaches upon that which is near it.[127]

"The turnings of the sun and moon in their course may be due to the obliquity of the heaven, whereby it is forced back at these times.[128] Again, they may equally be due to the contrary pressure of the air or, it may be, to the fact that either the fuel from time to time necessary has been consumed in the vicinity or there is a dearth of it. Or even because such a whirling motion was from the first inherent in these stars so that they move in a sort of spiral. For all such explanations and the like do not conflict with any clear evidence, if only in such details we hold fast to what is possible, and can bring each of these explanations into accord with the facts, unmoved by the servile artifices of the astronomers.

94. "The waning of the moon and again her waxing[129] might be due to the rotation of the moon's body, and equally well to configurations which the air assumes; further, it may be due to the interposition of certain bodies. In short, it may happen in any of the ways in which the facts within our experience suggest such an appearance to be explicable. But one must not be so much in love with the explanation by a single way as wrongly to reject all the others from ignorance of what can, and what cannot, be within human knowledge, and consequent longing to discover the indiscoverable. Further,

---

[126] Cf. Lucr. v. 509 f.

[127] From Lucr. v. 519 f. it is probable that words are lost from the text which ascribed these motions to the quest of fiery atoms by the heavenly bodies.

[128] Cf. Lucr. v. 614 f.

[129] Cf. Lucr. v. 705-750.

the moon may possibly shine by her own light, just as possibly she may derive her light from the sun;

95. for in our own experience we see many things which shine by their own light and many also which shine by borrowed light. And none of the celestial phenomena stand in the way, if only we always keep in mind the method of plural explanation and the several consistent assumptions and causes, instead of dwelling on what is inconsistent and giving it a false importance so as always to fall back in one way or another upon the single explanation. The appearance of the face in the moon may equally well arise from interchange of parts, or from interposition of something, or in any other of the ways which might be seen to accord with the facts.

96. For in all the celestial phenomena such a line of research is not to be abandoned; for, if you fight against clear evidence, you never can enjoy genuine peace of mind.

"An eclipse of the sun or moon may be due to the extinction of their light, just as within our own experience this is observed to happen; and again by interposition of something else — whether it be the earth or some other invisible body like it. And thus we must take in conjunction the explanations which agree with one another, and remember that the concurrence of more than one at the same time may not impossibly happen. [*He says the same in Book XII. of his "De Natura," and further that the sun is eclipsed when the moon throws her shadow over him, and the moon is eclipsed by the shadow of the earth; or again, eclipse may be due to the moon's withdrawal, and this is cited by Diogenes the Epicurean in the first book of his "Epilecta."*]

97. "And further, let the regularity of their orbits be explained in the same way as certain ordinary incidents within our own experience; the divine nature must not on any account be adduced to explain this, but must be kept free from the task and in perfect bliss. Unless this be done, the whole study of celestial phenomena will be in vain, as indeed it has proved to be with some who did not lay hold of a possible method, but fell into the folly of supposing that these events happen in one single way only and of rejecting all the others which are possible, suffering themselves to be carried into the realm of

the unintelligible, and being unable to take a comprehensive view of the facts which must be taken as clues to the rest.

98. "The variations in the length of nights and days may be due to the swiftness and again to the slowness of the sun's motion in the sky, owing to the variations in the length of spaces traversed and to his accomplishing some distances more swiftly or more slowly, as happens sometimes within our own experience; and with these facts our explanation of celestial phenomena must agree; whereas those who adopt only one explanation are in conflict with the facts and are utterly mistaken as to the way in which man can attain knowledge.

"The signs in the sky which betoken the weather may be due to mere coincidence of the seasons, as is the case with signs from animals seen on earth, or they may be caused by changes and alterations in the air. For neither the one explanation nor the other is in conflict with facts,

99. and it is not easy to see in which cases the effect is due to one cause or to the other.

"Clouds may form and gather either because the air is condensed under the pressure of winds, or because atoms which hold together and are suitable to produce this result become mutually entangled, or because currents collect from the earth and the waters; and there are several other ways in which it is not impossible for the aggregations of such bodies into clouds to be brought about. And that being so, rain may be produced from them sometimes by their compression, sometimes by their transformation;

100. or again may be caused by exhalations of moisture rising[130] from suitable places through the air, while a more violent inundation is due to certain accumulations suitable for such discharge. Thunder may be due to the rolling of wind in the hollow parts of the clouds, as it is sometimes imprisoned in vessels which we use; or to the roaring of fire in them when blown by a wind,[131] or to the rending and disruption of clouds, or to the friction and splitting up of clouds when they have become as firm as ice. As in the whole survey, so in this

---

[130] Lucr. vi. 519.
[131] Cf. Lucr. vi. 271-284.

particular point, the facts invite us to give a plurality of explanations.

101. Lightnings too happen in a variety of ways. For when the clouds rub against each other and collide, that collocation of atoms which is the cause of fire generates lightning; or it may be due to the flashing forth from the clouds, by reason of winds, of particles capable of producing this brightness; or else it is squeezed out of the clouds when they have been condensed either by their own action or by that of the winds; or again, the light diffused from the stars may be enclosed in the clouds, then driven about by their motion and by that of the winds, and finally make its escape from the clouds; or light of the finest texture may be filtered through the clouds (whereby the clouds may be set on fire and thunder produced), and the motion of this light may make lightning; or it may arise from the combustion of wind brought about by the violence of its motion and the intensity of its compression;

102. or, when the clouds are rent asunder by winds, and the atoms which generate fire are expelled, these likewise cause lightning to appear. And it may easily be seen that its occurrence is possible in many other ways, so long as we hold fast to facts and take a general view of what is analogous to them. Lightning precedes thunder, when the clouds are constituted as mentioned above and the configuration which produces lightning is expelled at the moment when the wind falls upon the cloud, and the wind being rolled up afterwards produces the roar of thunder; or, if both are simultaneous, the lightning moves with a greater velocity towards us

103. and the thunder lags behind, exactly as when persons who are striking blows are observed from a distance.[132] A thunderbolt is caused when winds are repeatedly collected, imprisoned, and violently ignited; or when a part is torn asunder and is more violently expelled downwards, the rending being due to the fact that the compression of the clouds has made the neighbouring parts more dense; or again it may be due like thunder merely to the expulsion of the

---

[132] E.g., as Apelt remarks, when the blows struck by a great hammer on a block of iron are watched from a distance, and it takes some time for the sound to reach one's ear.

imprisoned fire, when this has accumulated and been more violently inflated with wind and has torn the cloud, being unable to withdraw to the adjacent parts because it is continually more and more closely compressed — [*generally by some high mountain where thunderbolts mostly fall*].

104. And there are several other ways in which thunder-bolts may possibly be produced. Exclusion of myth is the sole condition necessary; and it will be excluded, if one properly attends to the facts and hence draws inferences to interpret what is obscure.

"Fiery whirlwinds are due to the descent of a cloud forced downwards like a pillar by the wind in full force and carried by a gale round and round, while at the same time the outside wind gives the cloud a lateral thrust; or it may be due to a change of the wind which veers to all points of the compass as a current of air from above helps to force it to move; or it may be that a strong eddy of winds has been started and is unable to burst through laterally because the air around is closely condensed.

105. And when they descend upon land, they cause what are called tornadoes, in accordance with the various ways in which they are produced through the force of the wind; and when let down upon the sea, they cause waterspouts.

"Earthquakes may be due to the imprisonment of wind underground, and to its being interspersed with small masses of earth and then set in continuous motion, thus causing the earth to tremble. And the earth either takes in this wind from without or from the falling in of foundations, when undermined, into subterranean caverns, thus raising a wind in the imprisoned air. Or they may be due to the propagation of movement arising from the fall of many foundations and to its being again checked when it encounters the more solid resistance of earth.

106. And there are many other causes to which these oscillations of the earth may be due.

"Winds arise from time to time when foreign matter continually and gradually finds its way into the air; also through the gathering of great store of water. The rest of the winds arise when a few of them fall into the many hollows and they are thus divided and multiplied.

"Hail is caused by the firmer congelation and complete transformation, and subsequent distribution into drops, of certain particles resembling wind: also by the slighter congelation of certain particles of moisture and the vicinity of certain particles of wind which at one and the same time forces them together and makes them burst, so that they become frozen in parts and in the whole mass.

107. The round shape of hailstones is not impossibly due to the extremities on all sides being melted and to the fact that, as explained, particles either of moisture or of wind surround them evenly on all sides and in every quarter, when they freeze.

"Snow may be formed when a fine rain issues from the clouds because the pores are symmetrical and because of the continuous and violent pressure of the winds upon clouds which are suitable; and then this rain has been frozen on its way because of some violent change to coldness in the regions below the clouds. Or again, by congelation in clouds which have uniform density a fall of snow might occur through the clouds which contain moisture being densely packed in close proximity to each other; and these clouds produce a sort of compression and cause hail, and this happens mostly in spring.

108. And when frozen clouds rub against each other, this accumulation of snow might be thrown off. And there are other ways in which snow might be formed.

"Dew is formed when such particles as are capable of producing this sort of moisture meet each other from the air: again by their rising from moist and damp places, the sort of place where dew is chiefly formed, and their subsequent coalescence, so as to create moisture and fall downwards, just as in several cases something similar is observed to take place under our eyes.

109. And the formation of hoar-frost is not different from that of dew, certain particles of such a nature becoming in some such way congealed owing to a certain condition of cold air.

"Ice is formed by the expulsion from the water of the circular, and the compression of the scalene and acute-angled atoms contained in it; further by the accretion of such atoms from without, which being driven together cause the water to solidify after the expulsion of a certain number of round atoms.

"The rainbow arises when the sun shines upon humid air; or again by a certain peculiar blending of light with air, which will cause either all the distinctive qualities of these colours or else some of them belonging to a single kind, and from the reflection of this light the air all around will be coloured as we see it to be, as the sun shines upon its parts.

110. The circular shape which it assumes is due to the fact that the distance of every point is perceived by our sight to be equal; or it may be because, the atoms in the air or in the clouds and deriving from the sun having been thus united, the aggregate of them presents a sort of roundness.

"A halo round the moon arises because the air on all sides extends to the moon; or because it equably raises upwards the currents from the moon so high as to impress a circle upon the cloudy mass and not to separate it altogether; or because it raises the air which immediately surrounds the moon symmetrically from all sides up to a circumference round her and there forms a thick ring.

111. And this happens at certain parts either because a current has forced its way in from without or because the heat has gained possession of certain passages in order to effect this.

"Comets arise either because fire is nourished in certain places at certain intervals in the heavens, if circumstances are favourable; or because at times the heaven has a particular motion above us so that such stars appear; or because the stars themselves are set in motion under certain conditions and come to our neighbourhood and show themselves. And their disappearance is due to the causes which are the opposite of these.

112. Certain stars may revolve without setting not only for the reason alleged by some, because this is the part of the world round which, itself unmoved, the rest revolves, but it may also be because a circular eddy of air surrounds this part, which prevents them from travelling out of sight like other stars; or because there is a dearth of necessary fuel farther on, while there is abundance in that part where they are seen to be.

Moreover there are several other ways in which this might be brought about, as may be seen by anyone capable of reasoning in accordance with the facts. The wanderings of certain stars, if such wandering is their actual motion,

113. and the regular movement of certain other stars, may be accounted for by saying that they originally moved in a circle and were constrained, some of them to be whirled round with the same uniform rotation and others with a whirling motion which varied; but it may also be that according to the diversity of the regions traversed in some places there are uniform tracts of air, forcing them forward in one direction and burning uniformly, in others these tracts present such irregularities as cause the motions observed. To assign a single cause for these effects when the facts suggest several causes is madness and a strange inconsistency; yet it is done by adherents of rash astronomy, who assign meaningless causes for the stars whenever they persist in saddling the divinity with burdensome tasks.

114. That certain stars are seen to be left behind by others may be because they travel more slowly, though they go the same round as the others; or it may be that they are drawn back by the same whirling motion and move in the opposite direction; or again it may be that some travel over a larger and others over a smaller space in making the same revolution. But to lay down as assured a single explanation of these phenomena is worthy of those who seek to dazzle the multitude with marvels.

"Falling stars, as they are called, may in some cases be due to the mutual friction of the stars themselves, in other cases to the expulsion of certain parts when that mixture of fire and air takes place which was mentioned when we were discussing lightning;

115. or it may be due to the meeting of atoms capable of generating fire, which accord so well as to produce this result, and their subsequent motion wherever the impulse which brought them together at first leads them; or it may be that wind collects in certain dense mist-like masses and, since it is imprisoned, ignites and then bursts forth upon whatever is round about it, and is carried to that place to which its motion

impels it. And there are other ways in which this can be brought about without recourse to myths.

"The fact that the weather is sometimes foretold from the behaviour of certain animals is a mere coincidence in time.[133] For the animals offer no necessary reason why a storm should be produced; and no divine being sits observing when these animals go out and afterwards fulfilling the signs which they have given.

116. For such folly as this would not possess the most ordinary being if ever so little enlightened, much less one who enjoys perfect felicity.

"All this, Pythocles, you should keep in mind; for then you will escape a long way from myth, and you will be able to view in their connexion the instances which are similar to these. But above all give yourself up to the study of first principles and of infinity and of kindred subjects, and further of the standards and of the feelings and of the end for which we choose between them. For to study these subjects together will easily enable you to understand the causes of the particular phenomena. And those who have not fully accepted this, in proportion as they have not done so, will be ill acquainted with these very subjects, nor have they secured the end for which they ought to be studied."

117. Such are his views on celestial phenomena.

But as to the conduct of life, what we ought to avoid and what to choose, he writes as follows.[134] Before quoting his words, however, let me go into the views of Epicurus himself and his school concerning the wise man.

---

[133] Cf. 98, The same topic is now treated again. Usener, who attributed this whole epistle to a compiler, believed that both passages were taken from the same part of Epicurus's *On Nature*.

[134] Between the letter to Pythocles and that to Menoeceus come excerpts (117-120) dealing with the wise man as conceived by Epicurus, to which are added (120, 121) some ethical tenets.

There are three motives to injurious acts among men — hatred, envy, and contempt; and these the wise man overcomes by reason. Moreover, he who has once become wise never more assumes the opposite habit, not even in semblance, if he can help it. He will be more susceptible of emotion than other men: that will be no hindrance to his wisdom. However, not every bodily constitution nor every nationality would permit a man to become wise.

Even on the rack the wise man is happy. He alone will feel gratitude towards friends, present and absent alike, and show it by word and deed.

118. When on the rack, however, he will give vent to cries and groans. As regards women he will submit to the restrictions imposed by the law, as Diogenes says in his epitome of Epicurus' ethical doctrines. Nor will he punish his servants; rather he will pity them and make allowance on occasion for those who are of good character. The Epicureans do not suffer the wise man to fall in love; nor will he trouble himself about funeral rites; according to them love does not come by divine inspiration: so Diogenes in his twelfth book. The wise man will not make fine speeches. No one was ever the better for sexual indulgence, and it is well if he be not the worse.

119. Nor, again, will the wise man marry and rear a family: so Epicurus says in the *Problems* and in the *De Natura*. Occasionally he may marry owing to special circumstances in his life. Some too will turn aside from

their purpose. Nor will he drivel, when drunken: so Epicurus says in the *Symposium*. Nor will he take part in politics, as is stated in the first book *On Life*; nor will he make himself a tyrant; nor will he turn Cynic (so the second book *On Life* tells us); nor will he be a mendicant. But even when he has lost his sight, he will not withdraw himself[135] from life: this is stated in the same book. The wise man will also feel grief, according to Diogenes in the fifth book of his *Epilecta*.

120a. And he will take a suit into court. He will leave written words behind him, but will not compose panegyric. He will have regard to his property and to the future. He will be fond of the country. He will be armed against fortune and will never give up a friend. He will pay just so much regard to his reputation as not to be looked down upon. He will take more delight than other men in state festivals.[136]

121b.[137] The wise man will set up votive images. Whether he is well off or not will be matter of indifference to him. Only the wise man will be able to converse correctly about music and poetry, without however actually writing poems himself. One wise man does not move more wisely than another. And he will make money, but only by his wisdom, if he should be in poverty, and he will pay court to a king, if need be. He

---

[135] I.e. by suicide, as recommended by the Stoics (*supra*, vii. 130).
[136] Cf. Philodemus, Περὶ εὐσεβείας (Us. p. 258).
[137] The transposition of this paragraph is due to Bignone (p. 214, notes 2, 4).

will be grateful to anyone when he is corrected. He will found a school, but not in such a manner as to draw the crowd after him; and will give readings in public, but only by request. He will be a dogmatist but not a mere sceptic; and he will be like himself even when asleep. And he will on occasion die for a friend.

120b. The school holds that sins are not all equal; that health is in some cases a good, in others a thing indifferent; that courage is not a natural gift but comes from calculation of expediency; and that friendship is prompted by our needs. One of the friends, however, must make the first advances (just as we have to cast seed into the earth), but it is maintained by a partnership in the enjoyment of life's pleasures.

121a. Two sorts of happiness can be conceived, the one the highest possible, such as the gods enjoy, which cannot be augmented, the other admitting addition and subtraction of pleasures. We must now proceed to his letter.

"Epicurus to Menoeceus, greeting.

122.

> "Let no one be slow to seek wisdom when he is young nor weary in the search thereof when he is grown old. For no age is too early or too late for the health of the soul. And to say that the season for studying philosophy has not yet come, or that it is past and gone, is like saying that the season for happiness is not yet or that it is now no more. Therefore, both old and young ought to seek wisdom, the former in order that, as age comes over him, he may be young in good things because of the grace of what has been, and the latter in order

that, while he is young, he may at the same time be old, because he has no fear of the things which are to come. So we must exercise ourselves in the things which bring happiness, since, if that be present, we have everything, and, if that be absent, all our actions are directed toward attaining it.

123. "Those things which without ceasing I have declared unto thee, those do, and exercise thyself therein, holding them to be the elements of right life. First believe that God is a living being immortal and blessed, according to the notion of a god indicated by the common sense of mankind; and so believing, thou shalt not affirm of him aught that is foreign to his immortality or that agrees not with blessedness, but shalt believe about him whatever may uphold both his blessedness and his immortality. For verily there are gods, and the knowledge of them is manifest; but they are not such as the multitude believe, seeing that men do not steadfastly maintain the notions they form respecting them. Not the man who denies the gods worshipped by the multitude, but he who affirms of the gods what the multitude believes about them is truly impious.

124. For the utterances of the multitude about the gods are not true preconceptions but false assumptions; hence it is that the greatest evils happen to the wicked and the greatest blessings happen to the good from the hand of the gods, seeing that they are always favourable to their own good qualities and take pleasure in men like unto themselves, but reject as alien whatever is not of their kind.

"Accustom thyself to believe that death is nothing to us, for good and evil imply sentience, and death is the privation of all sentience; therefore a right understanding that death is nothing to us makes the mortality of life enjoyable, not by adding to life an illimitable time, but by taking away the yearning after immortality.

125. For life has no terrors for him who has thoroughly apprehended that there are no terrors for him in ceasing to live. Foolish, therefore, is the man who says that he fears death, not because it will pain when it comes, but because it pains in the prospect. Whatsoever causes no annoyance when it is present, causes only a groundless pain in the expectation. Death, therefore, the most awful of evils, is nothing to us, seeing that, when we are, death is not come, and, when death is come, we are not. It is nothing, then, either to the living or to the dead, for with the living it is not and the dead exist no longer.[138] But in the world, at one time men shun death as the greatest of all evils, and at another time choose it as a respite from the evils in life.

126. The wise man does not deprecate life nor does he fear the cessation of life. The thought of life is no offence to him, nor is the cessation of life regarded as an evil. And even as men choose of food not merely and simply the larger portion, but the more pleasant, so the wise seek to enjoy the time which is most pleasant and not merely that which is longest. And he who admonishes the young to live well and the old to make a good end speaks foolishly, not merely because of the desirableness of life, but because the same exercise at once teaches to live well and to die well. Much worse is he who says that it were good not to be born, but when once one is born to pass with all speed through the gates of Hades.[139]

127. For if he truly believes this, why does he not depart from life? It were easy for him to do so, if once he were firmly convinced. If he speaks only in mockery, his words are foolishness, for those who hear believe him not.

---

[138] The striking resemblance to this passage of ps.-Plat. *Axiochus*, 369 b, has often been pointed out, most recently by E. Chevallier, *Etude crit. du dialogue ps.-plat. L'Axiochos* (Lyon, 1914, pp. 74 sq.); he rightly maintains the priority of the letter to Menoeceus (ib. p. 76).
[139] Theognis 425, 427.

"We must remember that the future is neither wholly ours nor wholly not ours, so that neither must we count upon it as quite certain to come nor despair of it as quite certain not to come.

"We must also reflect that of desires some are natural, others are groundless; and that of the natural some are necessary as well as natural, and some natural only. And of the necessary desires some are necessary if we are to be happy, some if the body is to be rid of uneasiness, some if we are even to live.

128. He who has a clear and certain understanding of these things will direct every preference and aversion toward securing health of body and tranquillity of mind, seeing that this is the sum and end of a blessed life. For the end of all our actions is to be free from pain and fear, and, when once we have attained all this, the tempest of the soul is laid; seeing that the living creature has no need to go in search of something that is lacking, nor to look for anything else by which the good of the soul and of the body will be fulfilled. When we are pained because of the absence of pleasure, then, and then only, do we feel the need of pleasure. Wherefore we call pleasure the alpha and omega of a blessed life. Pleasure is our first and kindred good.

129. It is the starting-point of every choice and of every aversion, and to it we come back, inasmuch as we make feeling the rule by which to judge of every good thing. And since pleasure is our first and native good, for that reason we do not choose every pleasure whatsoever, but ofttimes pass over many pleasures when a greater annoyance ensues from them. And ofttimes we consider pains superior to pleasures when submission to the pains for a long time brings us as a consequence a greater pleasure. While therefore all pleasure because it is naturally akin to us is good, not all pleasure is choiceworthy, just as all pain is an evil and yet not all pain is to be shunned.

130. It is, however, by measuring one against another, and by looking at the conveniences and inconveniences, that all these matters must be judged. Sometimes we treat the good as an evil, and the evil, on the contrary, as a good. Again, we regard independence of outward things as a great good, not so as in all cases to use little, but so as to be contented with little if we have not much, being honestly persuaded that they have the sweetest enjoyment of luxury who stand least in need of it, and that whatever is natural is easily procured and only the vain and worthless hard to win. Plain fare gives as much pleasure as a costly diet, when once the pain of want has been removed,

131. while bread and water confer the highest possible pleasure when they are brought to hungry lips. To habituate one's self, therefore, to simple and inexpensive diet supplies all that is needful for health, and enables a man to meet the necessary requirements of life without shrinking, and it places us in a better condition when we approach at intervals a costly fare and renders us fearless of fortune.

"When we say, then, that pleasure is the end and aim, we do not mean the pleasures of the prodigal or the pleasures of sensuality, as we are understood to do by some through ignorance, prejudice, or wilful misrepresentation. By pleasure we mean the absence of pain in the body and of trouble in the soul.

132. It is not an unbroken succession of drinking-bouts and of revelry, not sexual love, not the enjoyment of the fish and other delicacies of a luxurious table, which produce a pleasant life; it is sober reasoning, searching out the grounds of every choice and avoidance, and banishing those beliefs through which the greatest tumults take possession of the soul. Of all this the beginning and the greatest good is prudence. Wherefore prudence is a more precious thing even than philosophy; from it spring all the other virtues, for it teaches that we cannot lead a life of pleasure which is not also a life of prudence, honour, and justice; nor lead a life of prudence,

honour, and justice, which is not also a life of pleasure. For the virtues have grown into one with a pleasant life, and a pleasant life is inseparable from them.

133. "Who, then, is superior in thy judgement to such a man? He holds a holy belief concerning the gods, and is altogether free from the fear of death. He has diligently considered the end fixed by nature, and understands how easily the limit of good things can be reached and attained, and how either the duration or the intensity of evils is but slight. Destiny, which some introduce as sovereign over all things, he laughs to scorn, affirming rather that some things happen of necessity, others by chance, others through our own agency. For he sees that necessity destroys responsibility and that chance or fortune is inconstant; whereas our own actions are free, and it is to them that praise and blame naturally attach.

134. It were better, indeed, to accept the legends of the gods than to bow beneath that yoke of destiny which the natural philosophers have imposed. The one holds out some faint hope that we may escape if we honour the gods, while the necessity of the naturalists is deaf to all entreaties. Nor does he hold chance to be a god, as the world in general does, for in the acts of a god there is no disorder; nor to be a cause, though an uncertain one, for he believes that no good or evil is dispensed by chance to men so as to make life blessed, though it supplies the starting-point of great good and great evil. He believes that the misfortune of the wise is better than the prosperity of the fool.

135. It is better, in short, that what is well judged in action should not owe its successful issue to the aid of chance.

"Exercise thyself in these and kindred precepts day and night, both by thyself and with him who is like unto thee; then never, either in waking or in dream, wilt thou be disturbed, but wilt live as a god among men. For man loses all semblance of mortality by living in the midst of immortal blessings."

Elsewhere he rejects the whole of divination,[140] as in the short epitome, and says, "No means of predicting the future really exists, and if it did, we must regard what happens according to it as nothing to us."

Such are his views on life and conduct; and he has discoursed upon them at greater length elsewhere.

136. He differs from the Cyrenaics[141] with regard to pleasure. They do not include under the term the pleasure which is a state of rest, but only that which consists in motion. Epicurus admits both; also pleasure of mind as well as of body, as he states in his work *On Choice and Avoidance* and in that *On the Ethical End*, and in the first book of his work *On Human Life* and in the epistle to his philosopher friends in Mytilene. So also Diogenes in the seventeenth book of his *Epilecta*, and Metrodorus in his Timocrates, whose actual words are: "Thus pleasure being conceived both as that species which consists in motion and that which is a state of rest." The words of Epicurus in his work On Choice are: "Peace of mind and freedom from pain are pleasures which imply a state of rest; joy and delight are seen to consist in motion and activity."

137. He further disagrees with the Cyrenaics in that they hold that pains of body are worse than mental pains; at all events evil-doers are made to suffer bodily punishment; whereas Epicurus holds the pains of the mind to be the worse; at any rate the flesh endures the

---

[140] This short note on divination is clumsily inserted between the last words of the epistle and the expositor's natural reference to other works of Epicurus treating of ethics; Usener conjectures that it may have come from a Scholium attached to the epistle.
[141] Next come excerpts dealing with the difference between Epicurean and Cyrenaic ethics.

Life of Epicurus

storms of the present alone, the mind those of the past and future as well as the present. In this way also he holds mental pleasures to be greater than those of the body. And as proof that pleasure is the end he adduces the fact that living things, so soon as they are born, are well content with pleasure and are at enmity with pain, by the prompting of nature and apart from reason. Left to our own feelings, then, we shun pain; as when even Heracles, devoured by the poisoned robe, cries aloud,

> And bites and yells, and rock to rock resounds,
> Headlands of Locris and Euboean cliffs.[142]

138. And we choose the virtues too on account of pleasure and not for their own sake, as we take medicine for the sake of health. So too in the twentieth book of his *Epilecta* says Diogenes, who also calls education ἀγωγή recreation διαγωγή. Epicurus describes virtue as the sine qua non of pleasure, i.e. the one thing without which pleasure cannot be, everything else, food, for instance, being separable, i.e. not indispensable to pleasure.

Come, then, let me set the seal, so to say, on my entire work as well as on this philosopher's life by citing his *Sovran Maxims*,[143] therewith bringing the whole work to

---

[142] Soph. *Trach.* 787 f.; but our mss. read βοῶν for δάκνων.

[143] This collection of forty of the most important articles of faith in the Epicurean creed was famous in antiquity. It consists of extracts from the voluminous writings of Epicurus, and may have been put together by a faithful disciple. On the other hand, Epicurus laid great stress (35, 36) on epitomes of his doctrine being committed to memory; so that his passion

a close and making the end of it to coincide with the beginning of happiness.

1. 139. A blessed and eternal being has no trouble himself and brings no trouble upon any other being; hence he is exempt from movements of anger and partiality, for every such movement implies weakness [*Elsewhere he says that the gods are discernible by reason alone, some being numerically distinct, while others result uniformly from the continuous influx of similar images directed to the same spot and in human form.*]

2. Death is nothing to us; for the body, when it has been resolved into its elements, has no feeling, and that which has no feeling is nothing to us.

3. The magnitude of pleasure reaches its limit in the removal of all pain. When pleasure is present, so long as it is uninterrupted, there is no pain either of body or of mind or of both together.

4. 140. Continuous pain does not last long in the flesh; on the contrary, pain, if extreme, is present a very short time, and even that degree of pain which barely outweighs pleasure in the flesh does not last for many days together. Illnesses of long duration even permit of an excess of pleasure over pain in the flesh.

5. It is impossible to live a pleasant life without living wisely and well and justly, and it is impossible to live wisely and well and justly without living pleasantly.

---

for personal direction and supervision of the studies of his pupils may have induced him to furnish them with such an indispensable catechism.

Whenever any one of these is lacking, when, for instance, the man is not able to live wisely, though he lives well and justly, it is impossible for him to live a pleasant life.

6. In order to obtain security from other men any means whatsoever of procuring this was a natural good.[144]

7. 141. Some men have sought to become famous and renowned, thinking that thus they would make themselves secure against their fellow-men. If, then, the life of such persons really was secure, they attained natural good; if, however, it was insecure, they have not attained the end which by nature's own prompting they originally sought.

8. No pleasure is in itself evil, but the things which produce certain pleasures entail annoyances many times greater than the pleasures themselves.

9. 142. If all pleasure had been capable of accumulation, — if this had gone on not only by recurrence in time, but all over the frame or, at any rate, over the principal parts of man's nature, there would never have been any difference between one pleasure and another, as in fact there is.

10. If the objects which are productive of pleasures to profligate persons really freed them from fears of the mind, — the fears, I mean, inspired by celestial and

---

[144] Usener, followed by Bignone, regards ἀρχῆς καὶ βασιλείας of the vulgate text as a marginal gloss on ἐξ ὧν.

atmospheric phenomena, the fear of death, the fear of pain; if, further, they taught them to limit their desires, we should never have any fault to find with such persons, for they would then be filled with pleasures to overflowing on all sides and would be exempt from all pain, whether of body or mind, that is, from all evil.

11. If we had never been molested by alarms at celestial and atmospheric phenomena, nor by the misgiving that death somehow affects us, nor by neglect of the proper limits of pains and desires, we should have had no need to study natural science.

12. 143. It would be impossible to banish fear on matters of the highest importance, if a man did not know the nature of the whole universe, but lived in dread of what the legends tell us. Hence without the study of nature there was no enjoyment of unmixed pleasures.

13. There would be no advantage in providing security against our fellow-men, so long as we were alarmed by occurrences over our heads or beneath the earth or in general by whatever happens in the boundless universe.

14. When tolerable security against our fellow-men is attained, then on a basis of power sufficient to afford support[145] and of material prosperity arises in most genuine form the security of a quiet private life withdrawn from the multitude.

---

[145] Or, if ἐξοριστικῇ be read (with Meib., Kochalsky, and Apelt, cf.154), "power to expel."

15. 144. Nature's wealth at once has its bounds and is easy to procure; but the wealth of vain fancies recedes to an infinite distance.

16. Fortune but seldom interferes with the wise man; his greatest and highest interests have been, are, and will be, directed by reason throughout the course of his life.

17. The just man enjoys the greatest peace of mind, while the unjust is full of the utmost disquietude.

18. Pleasure in the flesh admits no increase when once the pain of want has been removed; after that it only admits of variation. The limit of pleasure in the mind, however, is reached when we reflect on the things themselves and their congeners which cause the mind the greatest alarms.

19. 145. Unlimited time and limited time afford an equal amount of pleasure, if we measure the limits of that pleasure by reason.

20. The flesh receives as unlimited the limits of pleasure; and to provide it requires unlimited time. But the mind, grasping in thought what the end and limit of the flesh is, and banishing the terrors of futurity, procures a complete and perfect life, and has no longer any need of unlimited time. Nevertheless it does not shun pleasure, and even in the hour of death, when ushered out of existence by circumstances, the mind does not lack enjoyment of the best life.

21. 146. He who understands the limits of life knows how easy it is to procure enough to remove the pain of want and make the whole of life complete and perfect. Hence he has no longer any need of things which are not to be won save by labour and conflict.

22. We must take into account as the end all that really exists and all clear evidence of sense to which we refer our opinions; for otherwise everything will be full of uncertainty and confusion.

23. If you fight against all your sensations, you will have no standard to which to refer, and thus no means of judging even those judgements which you pronounce false.

24. 147. If you reject absolutely any single sensation without stopping to discriminate with respect to that which awaits confirmation between matter of opinion and that which is already present, whether in sensation or in feelings or in any presentative perception of the mind, you will throw into confusion even the rest of your sensations by your groundless belief and so you will be rejecting the standard of truth altogether. If in your ideas based upon opinion you hastily affirm as true all that awaits confirmation as well as that which does not, you will not escape error, as you will be maintaining complete ambiguity whenever it is a case of judging between right and wrong opinion.

25. 148. If you do not on every separate occasion refer each of your actions to the end prescribed by nature, but instead of this in the act of choice or avoidance swerve

aside to some other end, your acts will not be consistent with your theories.

26. All such desires as lead to no pain when they remain ungratified are unnecessary, and the longing is easily got rid of, when the thing desired is difficult to procure or when the desires seem likely to produce harm.

27. Of all the means which are procured by wisdom to ensure happiness throughout the whole of life, by far the most important is the acquisition of friends.

28. The same conviction which inspires confidence that nothing we have to fear is eternal or even of long duration, also enables us to see that even in our limited conditions of life nothing enhances our security so much as friendship.

29. 149. Of our desires some are natural and necessary; others are natural, but not necessary; others, again, are neither natural nor necessary, but are due to illusory opinion. [*Epicurus regards as natural and necessary desires which bring relief from pain, as e.g. drink when we are thirsty; while by natural and not necessary he means those which merely diversify the pleasure without removing the pain, as e.g. costly viands; by the neither natural nor necessary he means desires for crowns and the erection of statues in one's honour. – Schol.*]

30. Those natural desires which entail no pain when not gratified, though their objects are vehemently pursued, are also due to illusory opinion; and when they are not

got rid of, it is not because of their own nature, but because of the man's illusory opinion.

31. 150. Natural justice is a symbol or expression of expediency, to prevent one man from harming or being harmed by another.

32. Those animals which are incapable of making covenants with one another, to the end that they may neither inflict nor suffer harm, are without either justice or injustice. And those tribes which either could not or would not form mutual covenants to the same end are in like case.

33. There never was an absolute justice, but only an agreement made in reciprocal intercourse in whatever localities now and again from time to time, providing against the infliction or suffering of harm.

34. 151. Injustice is not in itself an evil, but only in its consequence, viz. the terror which is excited by apprehension that those appointed to punish such offences will discover the injustice.

35. It is impossible for the man who secretly violates any article of the social compact to feel confident that he will remain undiscovered, even if he has already escaped ten thousand times; for right on to the end of his life he is never sure he will not be detected.

36. Taken generally, justice is the same for all, to wit, something found expedient in mutual intercourse; but in its application to particular cases of locality or conditions of whatever kind, it varies under different circumstances.

37. 152. Among the things accounted just by conventional law, whatever in the needs of mutual intercourse is attested to be expedient, is thereby stamped as just, whether or not it be the same for all; and in case any law is made and does not prove suitable to the expediencies of mutual intercourse, then this is no longer just. And should the expediency which is expressed by the law vary and only for a time correspond with the prior conception, nevertheless for the time being it was just, so long as we do not trouble ourselves about empty words, but look simply at the facts.

38. 153. Where without any change in circumstances the conventional laws, when judged by their consequences, were seen not to correspond with the notion of justice, such laws were not really just; but wherever the laws have ceased to be expedient in consequence of a change in circumstances, in that case the laws were for the time being just when they were expedient for the mutual intercourse of the citizens, and subsequently ceased to be just when they ceased to be expedient.

39. 154. He who best knew how to meet fear of external foes made into one family all the creatures he could; and those he could not, he at any rate did not treat as aliens; and where he found even this impossible, he avoided all intercourse, and, so far as was expedient, kept them at a distance.

40. Those who were best able to provide themselves with the means of security against their neighbours, being

thus in possession of the surest guarantee, passed the most agreeable life in each other's society; and their enjoyment of the fullest intimacy was such that, if one of them died before his time, the survivors did not lament his death as if it called for commiseration.

www.ingramcontent.com/pod-product-compliance
Lightning Source LLC
Chambersburg PA
CBHW020919090426
42736CB00008B/713